D1739180

Prescription for the Heart

Between Ignorance and Enlightenment (*II*)

By
Venerable Master Hsing Yun

Translated by
Venerable Miao Hsi and Cherry Lai

By Venerable Master Hsing Yun
Translated by Venerable Miao Hsi and Cherry Lai
Edited by Robin Stevens and Brenda Bolinger
Book designed by Ching Tay
Cover designed by Mei-Chi Shih

Published by Buddha's Light Publishing
3456 S. Glenmark Drive,
Hacienda Heights, CA 91745, U.S.A.
Tel: (626) 923-5143 - 5144 / (626) 961-9697
Fax: (626) 923-5145 / (626) 369-1944
E-mail: itc@blia.org
Website: www.blpusa.com

Library of Congress Cataloging-in-Publication Data

Xingyun, da shi.
  Prescription for the heart / By Venerable Master Hsing Yun ; translated by Ven. Miao Hsi and Cherry Lai ; edited by Robin Stevens.
      p. cm. -- (Between ignorance and enlightenment ; 2) Includes bibliographical references and index.
  ISBN 1-932293-02-7 (alk. paper)
  1. Conduct of life--Juvenile literature. 2. Buddhism--Social aspects--Juvenile literature. I. Hsi, Miao. II. Lai, Cherry. III. Stevens, Robin. IV. Title. V. Series. BJ1595.X55 2003 294.3'444--dc22
                                                    2003023777

Contents

Foreword

Since the inauguration of the daily paper, *The Merit Times,* in Taiwan on April 1, 2001, I have been writing an article each day for the column "Between Ignorance and Enlightenment." It is now nearly two years and I am still writing.

In the beginning, I was only trying it out, thinking I would finish in a couple of months. However, response from readers has been very enthusiastic, and I just could not stop writing.

According to the feedback from our readers, the staff at *The Merit Times* reported that many people subscribed to the paper because they wanted to read "Between Ignorance and Enlightenment." Some readers also indicated that after reading the column, their interests and skills in writing had improved. They were even able to gain acceptance to a university with their polished writing skills. Other readers made scrapbooks of the articles and used them as bedtime reading.

In addition, after reading the column some people who previously had numerous unwholesome habits have changed for the better. For instance, they have quit smoking, drinking, and gambling. There were also cases where family members had problems getting along with each other and they were inspired by the articles. Their families have become harmonious and joyful, filled with laughter and warmth. Some students wrote reports based on the articles and obtained high grades and commendation from their teachers.

These responses from different walks of life greatly reinforced my sense of duty for the column. Because of this mission, which I feel I must shoulder myself, I am motivated to write each and every day.

Regardless of how busy my schedule in propagating the Dharma may be, I can always find time during the day to make connections with the readers through my writing.

The English section of the American edition of the *Merit Times* is also publishing the articles translated by Hsi Lai Temple. Many study groups organized by members of the Buddha's Light International Association are using the articles for their discussions. Numerous readers have since called for a collective publication of these articles, and their earnest requests are now fulfilled.

The meaning of "Between Ignorance and Enlightenment" is actually reflected in our everyday life where there are inevitably many situations involving both "ignorance" and "enlightenment." Sometimes, those directly affected are deluded, while those around them may see through the situation very clearly. Therefore, a few appropriate words will be of much help in pointing the way to breakthrough, providing food for thought at the same time.

In reality, ignorance and enlightenment lie in just a thought! A thought of ignorance may cause sorrow and pain, while an instance of enlightenment can bring out the sun of wisdom. Just as Buddhist sutras indicate, "Troubles are Bodhi, and Bodhi is trouble!" The sourness of pineapples and grapes can be turned into sweetness with sunshine and warm breezes. Therefore, by being able to reflect and contemplate on the sourness of our ignorance, we can taste the sweetness of enlightenment right here and now.

This short publication is the second in a projected series of at least ten volumes. Through "Between Ignorance and Enlightenment," I wish to share and to grow with all my readers!

Hsing Yun

Preface

Between *Ignorance and Enlightenment*, Volume 2 is an inspiring collection of articles by Venerable Master Hsing Yun, which have been reprinted from his daily column in *The Merit Times* newspaper. He offers us a wide array of topics concerning our daily life, ranging from good health and longevity, the four seasons, and sleep to advertising, gossip, the empty nest syndrome, and extramarital affairs. Venerable Master Hsing Yun offers us hope and practical advice to address our universal problems living in a contemporary, technological world of "fast food culture." He uses down-to-earth language and ancient Chinese and Buddhist stories to convey his message. "Where there is hard work, nothing is impossible. Where there is diligence, there are benefits. Nothing is sweeter than the fruits of labor, but there will be no fruits if there is no labor. If we have a plot of fertile land, harvest will only be possible if we diligently till the earth and sow the seeds. These are the truths of everyday life."

Venerable Master Hsing Yun through his engaging articles shows us the way to turn our suffering into happiness in this troubled world. We must be willing "to face our shortcomings bravely and then change them for good." He also warns us about the trap of materialism that surrounds us today. "The most valuable thing in the world is not gold and emeralds, nor expensive cars and grand mansions, rather, it is the affinity between people."

He urges us to take the "middle path" in life, avoiding extremes in our thoughts, emotions, and actions, as well as to follow the Buddhists' Five Precepts. Joy is found not only through our diligence but also in our practice of contemplation, the cultivation of a positive attitude, and the building of good affinity with others. We enjoy and spread happiness when we are tolerant and open-minded and "show compassion, kindness, joy, and generosity" to others.

Venerable Master Hsing Yun's underlying theme in each article is always clear and uplifting. "Every one of us has unlimited potential; it all depends on whether we know how to develop it, and if we are willing to be an almighty person." The challenge is ours. We need only to see that "our emotions, successes and failures, or our lives in general" are within the grasp of our own hands. We should act as our own masters. As the saying goes, "'There is no natural born Sakyamuni, nor such a Maitreya.' Everything depends on our own efforts. As long as we strive toward our goals, we will be rewarded accordingly.... "

There is an enormous distance between ignorance and enlightenment. By reading and practicing the wisdom offered by Venerable Master Hsing Yun, hopefully we can find our own paths.

Marjorie Jacobs
Teacher and Counselor
Community Learning Center
Cambridge, Massachusetts
January 4th, 2002

Words from the Editor

*We own the whole universe in our minds
and embrace endless realms in our hearts.*

As we traverse the ups and downs of daily living in this modern world, we often find ourselves in need of inspiration and motivation. Rapid technological changes have created social upheavals in family structure and the way in which we live, creating stress in our lives that can often feel unbearable. We ask ourselves: how do we lead good, fulfilling lives? How do we face the constant barrage of violence and negativity in the media? How do we integrate spirituality into the fabric of our lives? As the quote above suggests, and as Buddhism teaches, the answers to these questions lie within each and every one of us.

First published in a daily column of *The Merit Times* newspaper, the articles in this collection were written by Venerable Master Hsing Yun, the charismatic founder of Fo Guang Shan Buddhist Order and the 48th Patriarch of the Linji (Rinzai) Chan School of Buddhism. Fo Guang Shan has grown from its roots as a small temple in Taiwan to one of the largest international Buddhist organizations in the world with branches worldwide.

Venerable Master Hsing Yun writes prolifically on Buddhist sutras and a wide spectrum of topics, spreading the Dharma, the teachings of Buddhism, to people everywhere. This work represents yet another effort to plant the seeds of Humanistic Buddhism in the path of every person, to bridge the gap between East and

West, and to enhance interfaith understanding and tolerance. Having dedicated his life to this cause, his writings are motivational and inspirational.

Written in Chinese and then translated and published in English, the short vignettes in this compilation are intended to instruct, motivate, inspire, and guide readers on their journey to spiritual discovery. They provide laypeople with introductory readings about the core teachings of Buddhism, teachings that can be applied to everyday living. The book can be read all at once or the articles read one at a time. The length of the articles lend themselves to quick and easy reading, yet they can be contemplated for hours afterward.

Through an examination of historical and current events, the articles in this book contextualize the basic teachings of Buddhism in the present, guiding us to open our minds and to practice compassion, magnanimity, and forbearance toward others. Using anecdotal evidence and examples from world and Buddhist history, we learn how Buddhist thinking can be applied to past events and continue to be relevant in the present as we confront modern problems, such as AIDS and the potential dangers of the Internet. We learn to seek out stories of kindness and inspiration in the media instead of only listening to the negative ones. We learn that through our own thoughts and actions we can affect our karma and that of others when we give good causes and conditions to others by offering encouragement and taking joy in their accomplishments. We are taught that small steps count toward the whole and that by simply changing our thinking and sharing joy with others we can improve our own paths.

Between Ignorance and Enlightenment is a stepping stone to meditation and other Buddhist practices. It is hoped that in reading these articles, the door to inquiry and discovery will be opened permanently and the teachings of Buddhism will become an integral part of daily living.

Robin Stevens

Acknowledgments

We received a lot of help from many people and we want to thank them for their efforts in making the publication of this book possible. We especially appreciate Venerable Tzu Jung, the Chief Executive of Fo Guang Shan International Translation Center (F.G.S.I.T.C.), Venerable Hui Chuan, the Abbot of Hsi Lai Temple, and Venerable Yi Chao, the Director of F.G.S.I.T.C. for their support and leadership; Venerable Miao Hsi and Cherry Lai for their translation; Robin Stevens and Brenda Bolinger for their editing; Dr. Tom Manzo for his proofreading; Mei-Chi Shih for her cover design and Ching Tay for her book design; Venerable Miao Han, Mae Chu, Mu-Tzen Hsu, Ching Tay, Echo Tsai, and Oscar Mauricio for preparing the manuscript for publication. Our appreciation also goes to everyone who has supported this project from its conception to its completion.

Prescription for the Heart

Between Ignorance and Enlightenment (*II*)

The Energy of Life

How much does the energy of life weigh? As the ancients described life and death, "Death could be as heavy as Mount Tai, or as light as a goose feather." What about the weight of life? It could also be as "Heavy as Mount Tai, or as light as a goose feather." Some live for three meals a day merely to keep themselves alive, and the value of their lives hinges on mealtimes; others strive in every way to benefit society, sometimes even shouldering the responsibility for world peace. It is easy to imagine how much their lives weigh.

In kidnapping cases, the value of the same human lives could be vastly different; the ransom for one could be a hundred thousand dollars, for another a million, and for yet another a billion! Some were born with a silver spoon in their mouths, and they simply live off their family's fortune. As they only spend their time in leisure, they fail to fully apply the energy of life. On the other hand, others may be born poor but are able to establish successful enterprises, benefiting society and the multitudes—such is the energy of their lives!

In undertaking endeavors in different professions, some may bear the burden of society's inequities. But once they reach the pinnacle, they become the focus of everyone's respect and admiration. Therefore, the energy of life lies in actualizing achievements and benefiting others. Regardless of age, both young and old can emit their life's energy just as effectively.

The energy of life is the true Buddha Nature, intrinsic in each person. Its discovery depends on the diligence and timing of the individual. For example, some may toil for decades in their careers without anyone paying attention to them. But once they have achieved success, they become renowned around the world. Others may feel trapped in their plight, yet, when opportunity surfaces, they rise to the top. The causes and conditions for reversing situations are very important.

The energy of life is endless, and its uses limitless. During the most recent world energy crisis, many of the world's nations looked for energy sources in the mountains and oceans, and even explored solar energy.

In reality, the source of energy lies within our minds. If we wish for our life energy to surge forth, we first need to discover its source. When the blind spots of our minds are eliminated, then the energy of wisdom, compassion, and merit will flow endlessly.

The Mahabodhi Temple where the
Sakyamuni Buddha achieved Buddhahood
is located in Bodhgaya, India

The Four Seasons of Life

Regardless of location in the world—be it the northern or southern hemisphere—most regions experience the changes of the four seasons—spring, summer, fall, and winter. Spring brings gentle breezes and showers, summer sees flourishing flowers and greenery, fall becomes dry and gusty, and winter gets cold and icy. The different climates of the four seasons can be likened to the various stages of life—each with its own characteristics.

A philosopher once compared life to the four seasons: youth is spring, adulthood is summer, middle age is fall, and old age is winter. Just as each season has its unique vista to offer, the four seasons of life also have their individual attributes. It is indeed an apt comparison.

Not only are there four stages to the seasons and life, in reality, all phenomena go through changes in each of the different phases. The universe goes through the four stages of formation, existence, decay, and emptiness. The world is born of causes and conditions, followed by a limited time of existence, and, as it goes through changes and increasing levels of decay, it finally ceases to exist. However, emptiness does not mean the end, because the world goes through the cycle of formation, existence, decay, and emptiness again and again, endlessly.

In reality, a human body also has four stages: birth, aging, sickness, and death. At birth, the entire household rejoices; in old age, loved ones are concerned; when sick, the mind worries; and upon death, the family grieves. But death does not spell the end of life. It is merely a transmigration; more rounds of birth, aging, sickness, and death will follow.

Our minds are also unceasingly going through stages of arising, abiding, changing, and extinction. When a thought arises, all sorts of vistas appear in our minds. While abiding, the mind flows on with the thought. But as the thought changes, a myriad of variations occur, and as it ceases, it wilts like a flower and waits for the next blossoming. We cannot control the four seasons of the world, nor the four phases of phenomena, but we can steer the wheel of the four seasons of life. So when they arrive, we should make the best use of them.

The spring of youth is the time to sprout and grow. We should fortify ourselves by absorbing nutrients, cultivating our compassion, and embracing the will to save the world. In the flourishing blossom of summer, we should benefit others by offering our energy to complement their growth. With the approaching maturity of fall, we should contribute what we know to the beginners in life by giving them the bountiful fruits that we have acquired. Upon the arrival of the winter of life, we should make use of our achievements to enrich the world, just as the winter sun warms the earth—what a wonderful finishing note to our lives that would be!

A human body has four stages: birth, aging, sickness, and death

A Positive View on Life

We all have different views on life. Some of us are optimistic, some pessimistic. The optimists think positively about everything they encounter, while the pessimists think negatively about everything they see.

However, there is no absolute optimism or pessimism in the world. "What arises in the mind gives rise to all dharmas, and all dharmas cease when the mind ceases." There are of course external causes and conditions for optimism and pessimism. But most of the time, they are the product of our own creation.

Once, a king went on a hunting excursion and accidentally broke his finger. When he asked the minister beside him what should be done, the latter was optimistic and answered lightheartedly, "This is a good thing!"

On hearing this, the king was furious. Blaming the minister for taking joy in his suffering, the king threw him in jail. A year later, the king went on another hunting trip and was captured by a band of natives. He was bound and put on the altar as an offering to the natives' deity. Just before the king was about to be offered, the high priest discovered that a finger was missing from his hand. Considered an incomplete offering, the king was set free and the minister accompanying him was used in his place.

The king thought of the jailed minister who had considered his broken finger a good thing and proceeded to set him free. Having jailed him for a year for no good reason, the king offered the minister his apology. However, the minister was still as optimistic as before and replied, "A year in jail is a good thing, too. If I were not in jail, who would have accompanied your highness on that hunting trip and been offered on the altar?"

Therefore, what is good is not necessarily all good. By the same token, what is bad is not necessarily all bad. Buddhism teaches impermanence. Things can change for the better or for the worse. Pessimists worry about the last million dollars they have left, while optimists are happy for the last thousand dollars they still own.

When the renowned scholar Su Dongpo was demoted to Hainan Island, he found the quiet solitude of the island a world apart from his former days of glory in the capital. Upon reflection, Su realized that he was not the only one living on a lone island in the universe. Even the continent itself is just another island in the vast ocean. Just like an ant climbing on a leaf floating in a tank of water, the leaf becomes its island. As a result, he simply accepted the circumstances and was happy with his lot. Whenever Su tasted the local seafood, he was happy that he lived in Hainan. He even thought that if other ministers had come before he had, he would not be able to enjoy all the delicious food by himself.

In thinking positively, life becomes truly joyful. Buddhist monastics have only the cassock on their backs and a pair of grass shoes on their feet. They travel about everywhere, like floating clouds. Keeping company with beggars or being in the presence of kings and emperors, they are equally comfortable. They are unfettered by anything, yet they own the dharma realms in their minds. In coexisting with all sentient beings of the universe, how could they be lonely?

Therefore, there is no absolute joy or suffering in life. As long as we have a positive attitude, the spirit to strive on, and the ability to think positively of what we encounter, suffering can be turned into joy, hardship into ease, and danger into safety. As Helen Keller once said, "In facing the sun, you will not see shadows." A positive view on life is indeed the sunshine in our hearts

The Enemies of Life

Enemies are those who oppose us, who obstruct us, who want to harm or even destroy us. However, the real enemy is our own selves. Why are we our own enemy? When we are lazy, laziness is our enemy; when we hate, hatred is our enemy; when we are selfish, selfishness is our enemy; and when we are dishonest, dishonesty is our enemy. Those who belittle righteousness see friends as enemies; those who are reluctant to share see relatives and friends as enemies. Those who do not care for their families will see their families as enemies. If the mind is not pure and morals are not established, one's own mind and body are one's enemies.

If we do not protect our own country but instead betray it, when our country is destroyed we would end up homeless. Are we not then our own enemy? If we do not make an effort at work, eventually our employers may no longer be able to continue doing business and close down, and we would be out of work. Are we not then our own enemy? For those who get drunk and cause trouble, are they not their own enemy? Or, when they become ill from their misguided living, are they not their own enemy?

We should befriend those who are wise, but if we are jealous of them, not only will we be unable to learn from them, we may even contribute to our own failure. When siblings are set to fight with each other, or those in the same company aim to destroy one another, it may appear that they are getting rid of the competition; in reality, they are weakening the team effort, as well as themselves as a whole.

According to the sutras, the demon is not outside; it is within our minds. Our minds nurture many enemies: greed, anger, delusion, pessimism, suspicion, arrogance, and worry. When the Fourth Patriarch Chan Master Daoxin first visited Chan Master Sengcan, Master Daoxin asked for the way to liberation. Master Sengcan replied with a question, "Who is restricting you?"

Master Daoxin thought for a while and replied, "No one."

Chan Master Sengcan then asked, "If no one is restricting you, then why do you need to be liberated?" This teaches us that we all restrict and bind our own selves.

Renowned scholar Wang Yangming once said, "It is easy to catch the bandit hiding in the mountains, but it is difficult to grab the thief inside the mind." External enemies are easy to confront; however, enemies from within our minds are harder to defeat. The *Diamond Sutra* states that we have to conquer our minds. If we can conquer our minds, then we can defeat our enemy, who is actually our own self.

Extramarital Affairs

People are born of love, and love enhances life. But love can also cause a lot of trouble, especially when it involves extramarital affairs that could wreck families and ruin people's reputations, causing much anguish and suffering. For a couple to love each other is a rare cause and condition. When two people find each other and fall in love, are recognized by others, and win the approval of both families to get married, it is indeed a wonderful event, deserving of blessing. However, life is impermanent, and if even just one party has an affair, then the couple's family, career, reputation, and even money will be all tangled up and many problems that are hard to resolve will ensue.

Why do people have affairs? There must be a reason for them. Once an affair occurs, it is useless to harp about the consequences; rather, it is more important to look at the cause. Those who are affected by extramarital affairs often blame the third party for disrupting the relationship. However, in addition to the third person, the couple is also responsible for the problem. For example, some people may be so busy at work or with their social life that they do not find time to look after their family and spouse, opening up a chance for a third person to come between the couple. Also, affairs can result from a couple's different outlooks or lifestyles, and even different levels of achievement.

At the start of an affair, there are always some signs that the other side should be aware of. However, if a couple does not care enough to make amends with love and consideration, but instead begins to find fault and to pick on each other, the consequences are predictably negative. Only love wins love; if hatred is the cause, how could the effect be love? Therefore, upon discovering that one's spouse is having an affair, the wise should be considerate and forgiving, and make an effort to move the other half by loving and caring for him or her even more than before, such that the spouse will realize how much he or she is loved. Over time, the philanderer will recognize the destructiveness and error of his or her behavior, and the couple can start a new life again.

Because both persons in a marriage are originally from different families, it is only natural that there are differences in personality, habits, and thinking. Even in the best of times, it is not easy to keep a relationship. Both persons must maintain communication, respect, and tolerance for each other to strengthen their relationship. All issues of their life together, especially those regarding their outlooks, or those related to their children's education, should be discussed openly and honestly. Also, both sides can develop similar hobbies, get to know each other's friends, and socialize together; or set up occasions to enhance the romance in their relationship. These are some of the ways to diminish the chance of having affairs. If their life together is filled with joy and laughter, the idea of having an affair will never occur in either person's mind.

For a couple to love each other is a
rare cause and condition

The Wrong Friends

The ancients said, "If one is to learn without friends, then one will become isolated and unlearned." The honorable will make friends based on principles, and the dishonorable will base friendships on advantages. People are always connected to their friendships based on circumstances. Confucianism considers "friendship" as one of life's five basic morals, meaning friendship should be guided by ethics as well. Friends are indeed an important part of life, as a Chinese saying goes, "One relies on one's parents when one is at home, and depends on one's friends when one is outside." The prospect of one's future is closely related to whether one's friends are right or not.

The *Foshuo Bei Sutra* states, "There are four kinds of friends: friends who are like flowers, friends who are like scales, friends who are like the mountains, and friends who are like the earth." Friends who are like flowers and scales are not the right friends. Friends who are like flowers will only cherish you when they want something from you. When you are no longer of use to them, they will desert you. Friends who are like scales will flatter you in good times, but when you are down in life, they will look down upon you. Therefore, friends should be like the mountains and earth, because they will always be there for you and support you through thick and thin.

Generally, people should look for these three qualities in their friends: that they are honest, understanding, and knowledgeable. But there are many kinds of friends: friends to go out and have fun with, friends to start a business with, friends to share hard times with, and even friends to be superficial with. Some people's lives change for the better because of friends, and conversely, others find themselves entrapped in dire situations because of friends. Therefore, one must be cautious in making friends.

Friends should not be jealous of each other's achievements or talents, as there are numerous cases where good friends have become enemies because of jealousy. Rather, friends should support and help each other to succeed. The most important things in friendship are honesty, cooperation, understanding, and trust. We should make friends with those who are willing to point out our faults and not those who are quick to flatter us with empty compliments. One will be very fortunate if there are even a few friends who are steadfast, loyal, supportive, and devoted. Otherwise, one may be better off to have no one, rather than to make friends who are calculating, insincere, or bent on taking advantage of others.

The ancients placed great importance on moral value in choosing friends. As Confucianism teaches, "One is stained red when close to vermilion and black when close to ink." Another saying goes, "When one makes the right friends, it is as though one has become oblivious to the fragrance of orchids after staying too long in their presence, and similarly, in making the wrong friends, it is as though one has become unaware of the stench of a fish market after spending too much time there." Friends should encourage each other to be kind and compassionate, not to be partners in crime. If one makes the wrong friends, one's life will be filled with peril. Should one not be cautious?

A Society of Advertisements

In the development of Chinese society, from the ancient time of nomadic tribes to agricultural villages, and from industrial towns of various levels, we have now progressed to the electronic community of today's computers. But in essence, what we have today is a society of advertisements.

Nowadays, no matter what people set out to do, they all need advertising to promote their work. The products manufactured by factories require advertisements for them to be introduced to the public. Whether it is people looking for work, or vacant positions in need of talent to fill them, advertisements are necessary. The sale of real estate property also needs to be advertised. Even personal matters, such as the passing of celebrities, the announcement of weddings, and sometimes even divorces are published for all to know. For those who want to air their grievances or those who wish to share their ideals with the world, the best channel for them to do so is through advertising in the media. Even governments rely on advertising to publish their policies, and little heard of countries also need advertisements to make themselves known to the world.

Advertising has already become a part of modern people's lives. Because of the financial support of advertisement, newspapers are published every day for all to read. In that respect, we really should be grateful for them. Similarly, while we are watching television we should not be turned off by the commercials, for without them, there would be no television programs available for us to enjoy. When we are shopping for our daily necessities, we should also be thankful for advertisements, for without them, we would have nothing to refer to about the latest products.

Religion integration is a kind of wonderful deed

Even in our leisure time, we might need to see commercials for the latest movies, should we wish to see one.

In the past, the Buddha was honored as "Transcendent Understanding of the Ordinary World." He did not need any infomercials and was able to know and understand every phenomenon. Ancient Chinese scholars, being so learned, were supposed "to know what is happening in the world without leaving home." But in today's life, we all need advertisements to learn about the world and what is going on in our society. Advertisements reflect the culture of the era and may even pioneer the developments of our time. Unfortunately, though, advertisements nowadays share a serious flaw. They are often exaggerated and unrealistic in their claims, thus losing the trust of the public and leading people to view advertisements as phony promotion.

If there is a certain phrase that has become popular, that particular phrase becomes a kind of advertisement. Or, if someone performed a certain deed that has become universally known, then this person is advertising for himself as well as for the nation. In enhancing industrial and commercial development, and advancing social prosperity, advertisements indeed carry a mission. However, we do wish that from now on, advertisements could regain a more realistic, pure nature in order to serve their true purpose in benefiting the populace.

The Abhorrence of Falsehood

Nowadays it seems to be common to speak falsely in order to win votes, or to give false evidence to put others in suffering, or to cheat in order to benefit oneself, or to falsify brand name products to make illegitimate profits. "False" seems to be all over the place. The perpetuators believe they can control everyone through their false speech, deceptive behavior, and fake manners. But in reality, no matter how "real" they appear to be, falsehoods can only last for the moment and not forever; there will always come a time when trickery is revealed.

Some may refute this by saying, "The world is made up of the four gross elements and the five aggregates, which by themselves are empty in nature. Since everything is 'false' anyway, why do we need to be so serious?" True, it is so, but if we dream in our dreams and behave deceptively in an unreal world, then where is our true nature? Where is the meaning of life? The world is filled with false speech and deceptive people. In the past women dressed up to be like men; nowadays both men and women cross-dress, and nobody can tell them apart. Only the innocent and simple-minded often become drunken and lost in the joy and pleasures of reality and falsehood.

Actually, regardless of time and space, falsehood and reality are all in the mind. Once, a rich merchant asked Mark Twain if he could tell which one of his eyes was artificial, and to his surprise, Mark Twain immediately pointed out that it was the left one. "Because there is not any kindness in your right eye, but there seem to be some real feelings in the left one" was his reasoning. His short reply satirizes the world's falsehoods. In today's world, the wind of falsehood is blowing everywhere; people cheat and deceive, fake and forge, lie and "fib." Many are cheated by fake emotions, deceived by false

Living in a world of falsehoods, are we not abhorrent?

speech. Living in a world of falsehoods, is this not abhorrent? Hopefully, educators and the media can lead the way in guiding society to speak the truth, to perform true deeds, and to hold true feelings. Then, maybe we will be able to liberate ourselves from drowning in a sea of falsehoods. Living in a world of falsehoods, are we not abhorrent.

The Abhorrence of Attachments

There are thousands of troubles in life. Physically, there are aging, sickness, and death; mentally, there are greed, hatred, and delusion. Among them, the most difficult to deal with is self-attachment, for it is the commander of eighty-four thousand troubles. Because of the attachment to "I" and "self," there are endless troubles caused by "I doubt, I envy, and I view."

Some are willing to give up all their material possessions in exchange for their lives because they are more attached to life. Then there are those who would forfeit morality in the face of fame and fortune, and that is due to their deviant attachment to ego and materialism. This illustrates the relationship between the attachment to gain and loss and those things that are closely related to the self. Also, because of our attachments, we find it difficult to change our bad habits and unwholesome speech. In life, we may have attachments to knowledge, views, and ideas; we will be fine if they are correct and reasonable. But if we are attached to speech and views that are devious, then others will find it difficult to tolerate us.

We should understand that in dealing with all phenomena in this world, "no rule is the rule," for we need to adjust and change. If this road is blocked, we need to reroute ourselves, and if this way does not work, then we have to find another way and should not stubbornly insist on our ideas. As the saying goes, "A stubborn mind is unable to complete anything." Those who have attachments are often too stubborn to change their ways and tend not to work well with others, are not able to "go with the flow," or cannot accept others' views.

Because of these character flaws, they experience difficulties in their careers and in interpersonal relationships. When it comes to "attachments," even though they may already have let go of the self, the enlightened saints would sometimes still have benign attachments to the Dharma. But should we be deluded into becoming attached to meaningless gossip, or the right and wrong between self and others, then it would be difficult for others to bear with us.

With "attachments" it is impossible for us to move on in life, for if we do not give up the last step, how are we going to take the next one? It is only when we give up our attachments that we are able to open up new vistas. The most difficult attachments of all to release are love and hatred; self-attachment and self-love, or self-grudge and self-view, are all sentiments that bring about deviant thinking and ideas, tightly binding us like ropes and creating endless trouble. A wondrous method that we can use to release ourselves from attachments is none other than the Buddhist teachings of prajna, wisdom, and contemplation; otherwise, how will we gain liberation and ease?

We should let go of the raft when we arrive at the bank

The Malice of Gossip

There is gossip every day, but it seems to be especially prevalent in today's society. Be it in the family, the community, between friends, siblings, or spouses, we are all troubled by malice.

We could all actually live a happy wonderful life if gossip would never inflict us like a disease. Sometimes there seems to be nowhere to hide from it. As the saying goes, "Good news may not be able to go anywhere, while bad news spreads a thousand miles." This only proves the unsurpassed power of gossip.

Some paint a bad picture of the good deeds of others and portray a good one of their own faults, purposely confusing right with wrong so that those around them are unable to grasp reality and therefore cannot understand the truth. What is right and wrong can easily be mixed up with gossip, and many find it difficult to separate the two. As long as someone says, "We all say so," or, "Other people are saying so, and they are absolutely sure about it," then gossip can become established as truth.

Buddhism classifies lying, duplicity, harsh speech, and meaningless speech as "gossip." Internationally, powerful countries are "right" while weaker ones are "wrong"; in society, the wealthy are "right" while those in poverty are "wrong." Then there are those with ulterior motives; they create tempests in a teacup by clouding the distinction between right and wrong simply through the strength of their words. Nowadays, some of the media go to extremes to create sensationalism, and thus mislead the public.

Consequently, some become so aggravated that they can no longer find peace and stability in life, while others lose what they have achieved by being ensnared in gossip. We often say that when

A lie spoken thirty times will become the truth

a lie is repeated three times by three different people, it will then start to sound like the truth. There is a famous communist saying, "A lie spoken thirty times will become the truth." Lies and gossip are indeed malicious!

However, people in this world are not really disregarding the truth. As the saying goes, "The heavens are watching what people are doing and listening to what they are saying." In the course of worldly affairs, the truth of the universe will always hold its place and cannot be altered; just as cause and effect are unchangeable, so is the truth. "People may take advantage of the kindly, but the heavens will not; people may fear the vicious, but the heavens will not." In the face of cause and effect, the reality of the truth will be revealed and justice will ultimately be done.

Right and wrong, good and evil, cause and effect; all of these are clear and distinct. It is truly regrettable that many cannot live in peace when inflicted with the negative effects of gossip, or may become so overwhelmed by it that they commit suicide to prove their innocence. But in reality, the distinction between guilt and innocence already exists clearly. Gossip ceases with the wise; we all should practice, "speak no gossip, hear no gossip, ignore all gossip, spread no gossip, and fear no gossip." Then, gossip would not trouble us anymore.

We should realize that anyone who arrives bearing gossip is the one spreading it, but as long as we have a clear conscience, we need not please everyone around us. If we only behave right, then we have nothing to fear in the face of gossip.

The Importance of Unity

The Chinese are often derided for their lack of unity; "as loose as a platter of sand," as the saying goes. Some say that three Japanese may establish a large conglomerate, and three Germans may run city hall, but three Chinese would mess up a family, because Chinese are better at working on their own. Consequently, nowadays some Chinese are promoting "team spirit" and "team work," emphasizing the importance of unity.

Unity is actually the union of causes and conditions! In building a house, it is not enough to have only steel and concrete; you need materials such as wood and mortar, as well as human resources and adequate space, before one can construct a building from the ground up. For a tree to grow big and tall, the "cause" of a seed alone is not enough for the tree to germinate. It also requires sunlight, air, water, and soil—the necessary "conditions" for it to grow into a large shady tree.

The rapid development of the world's computer industry is not just the achievement of a handful of entrepreneurs, for without the hard work and support of many researchers and workers in the field, it would be impossible to grow at the pace that it did. Regardless of the type of business, success is always the result of the effort and wisdom of many, and their concerted endeavor is the actualization of team spirit.

Unity is the willingness to contribute and support others, helping them to succeed in their enterprises. But it seems that many overseas Chinese tend to be critical of each other, often fighting with one another for various reasons. We are called "roosters" for our refusal to cooperate or to follow the lead of others. The Japanese, on the other hand, have the team spirit of "ducks," who follow directions and thus are able to travel the world, establishing communities.

Singapore is one of the "Four Little Dragons of Asia," but being a small country did not stop it from achieving the status of a developed country. Their success is again attributed to their team spirit. Looking back at China, it is a big country, but because of the emphasis placed on individuals and their personal abilities, the country's overall achievement is limited. When we study Chinese history, we see that the demise of the dynasties was almost always due to fighting between the emperor and his ministers, the betrayal of his relatives, or the rebellion of his subjects. If a business fails, it is often because of the lack of leadership and cooperation between its executives. Just like a person, if the mind cannot control the eyes, ears, nose, and tongue, then of course the overall spirit of that person is not fully unified. Therefore, we must understand that unity is strength, because with unity we possess an edge that will help us to succeed in any undertaking. Team spirit is a kind of unity.

Team spirit is a kind of unity

Harmony Between the Self and Others

Interpersonal relationships are a very important part of today's life, and many people are troubled and distressed because the relationship between the self and others is not in harmony. This is because they do not know how to deal with others, nor do they know how to cultivate the self. Or, they may try to further differentiate and distinguish the self from others, thus creating a multitude of problems and prompting even more improper behavior.

In reality, the relationship between the self and others is maintained by conditions, so good conditions bring about good friendships, and poor conditions result in bad karma. However, most people fail to realize the relationship between cause and effect. Not only are they unwilling to assist others in their tasks, but they also become envious of others' achievements, always calculating and comparing themselves with others and trying to devise a means to beat them in every circumstance. This often results in disharmony in relationships, further hurting the self and others and causing suffering.

For humans, once the thought of discriminating and comparing arises, or the intention to compare gains and losses surfaces, even those as close as loving family members begin to fight. Therefore, to cling to the "self" is the source of suffering; being "selfless" is the solution to the conflict between the self and others. There is fighting and injustice among people because the relationship between the self and others is in disharmony. So the only way to achieve harmony between people is to treat others as the self. When you and I are one and the same, then we can be truly considerate of each other's feelings, and we can consider matters from each other's point of view. This is the ultimate way to resolve our suffering.

Everyone would like to be better than other people, but because of this desire to excel, endless fighting ensues. On the other hand, if we respect one another's strengths, if we give each other support and assistance, then peace and harmony can be realized. Most would like to possess more than others and disregard the deficiencies that others may face;

but if you are the only one who is enjoying everything while everyone else has nothing, do you think they are going to leave you in peace?

Most of us prefer ease above hard work, pursuing joy and serenity for ourselves and disregarding the suffering of others. This is the source of fighting in the world. But if we give others joy, then we will be happy when others are joyful. Fighting for victory and shunning blame is a common ill and the basis of conflict, but if we are willing to admit our mistakes and faults, if we do not shrink from responsibility, the relationship between the self and others will be in harmony. Just remember, by simply retreating one step, we can broaden our vistas. The way to resolve conflicts between the self and others is to practice "you are big and I am small, you are right and I am wrong." When we can truly do that, then we will be able to attain unexpected Dharma joy.

Harmony between self and others in a chorus is very important

The Wonder of Being Disadvantaged

There is a saying, "To be disadvantaged is actually advantageous." But most would still like to be the one taking advantage, not the other way around. Since nobody likes to get the short end of the stick, those who always like to take advantage of others will surely be disliked. Therefore, in handling one's affairs and dealing with others, one should be willing to "be disadvantaged" because that is the best way to earn the respect and admiration of others and also the way to achieve success in life.

There have been many scams in society where people were defrauded of their life savings. But in reality, it is because they meant to take advantage of others, deluded by greed for some big fortune, that they end up suffering because of their actions. Conversely, some may be viewed as greatly disadvantaged in what they do, and yet end up being the real winners. In ancient China, the Great Yu, founder of the Xia Dynasty, was in charge of controlling floods. He was so caught up in his work that he was unable to go home even after passing the door three times. Because he worked for the welfare of his countrymen, they selected him to be their emperor.

There is a Chinese story about two ghosts ready to be reborn as humans. The Judgment King of Hell asked them each to choose if they would like to be reborn as a giver or a taker. Subsequently, the one who chose to be reborn as a giver was born into a wealthy family and lived a life of generous giving, whereas the other one was born a beggar and spent his life begging for a living.

The moral of the story is that if one knows how to give and is not concerned about being disadvantaged, then life will be full of richness. On the other hand, if one is calculating and only knows how to take and does not give anything in return, then life will surely be poor. Therefore, to take advantage does not necessarily result in an advantageous situation and vice versa; realistically, to be disadvantaged is the way to take advantage.

As long as one holds right views and right thoughts, follows the circumstances, and puts others' needs first, even if one may be disadvantaged for the moment, the principle of cause and effect will bring positive results in the end. This is simply because what one should get, one will receive, regardless of how things appear on the surface. The Chinese saying, "Fortune lies in disadvantages," is truly the essence of the wisdom of the ancients.

To Take Delight in Learning One's Own Mistakes

"Humans are not saints and sages, who could be faultless!" Since ancient times in China, benevolent rulers had the courage to "issue proclamations on one's own sins," and humble ministers were brave enough to "bear all faults on their shoulders." Great emperors and scholars alike took delight in learning about their shortcomings because the ability to admit one's own mistakes is a virtue.

Nowadays in society, there are many people, especially young people, who share a major flaw. They refuse to learn about their faults or admit their mistakes. Sometimes, even if only kind advice is provided, they instead merely explain their stand or deliberately attempt to cover up their mistakes, never admitting their faults. With such intention to pass blame and refusal to take advice, how are they going to accomplish anything and make any progress?

President Clinton's scandal with Monica Lewinsky created such a public uproar, but because he was finally willing to admit his faults and apologize to his countrymen, he was able to clear the dark clouds over his head and gain brightness in life again. Leaders are sometimes driven from their positions by the schemes of political enemies, but if they would only admit to their mistakes, public opinion would be in their favor and due justice would be served. However, Chinese political personalities share a common shortcoming; they will never admit their mistakes. Even among the populace, be it between parents and children, supervisors and subordinates, or even between friends, people rarely admit their faults.

It takes courage to admit one's mistakes. In the past, the Chinese were ridiculed as the "Sick Man of East Asia," but in reality, everyone is a coward when faced with the prospect of having to learn of and admit their mistakes! This is because most consider faults as shameful, and to admit them is the greatest humiliation. Confucianism teaches, "Knowing humility is proximate to courage." Therefore, it is the courageous who truly know shamefulness and humility. *The Way to Buddhahood* says, "One should be shameful of what one does not understand, of what one cannot achieve, and of what is impure." Therefore, when one is able to know shame and admit one's mistakes, then one is capable of cultivating the bodhi mind and walking on the path to Buddhahood.

The founding father of the Republic of China, Dr. Sun Yat-sen, did not give up on his attempt to revolutionize the country even after many failures, and he finally succeeded in overthrowing the Qing Dynasty and establishing the Republic. Confucius wrote, "When one is wrong, then one should not be afraid to correct it." Only if we can take delight in learning from our mistakes will we be able to correct them, for that is the way it should be.

To be able to admit one's mistakes is a virtue

The Importance of Making Affinity

The most valuable thing in the world is not gold and emeralds nor expensive cars and grand mansions; rather, it is the affinity between people. In order for people to get along, there needs to be affinity, and in order to achieve success, people and matters need to have affinity as well. Be it between people and society; matters and affairs; or you, me, and them; there needs to be affinity for anything to be done well.

The term "affinity" has a very deep meaning—to make affinity is to plant seeds, for without the planting of seeds, how could there be a harvest in the future? The deeper and broader the affinity, the bigger the deposit will be in the "bank account," and with a substantial "bank account" to support us, it will be easier to succeed in our endeavors. There are causes behind every success story in this world; so, should we wish to have a successful career, we need to have favorable causes and conditions.

There are those who are multibillionaires, but, if they do not have affinity with others, no matter where they go, they are disliked. On the other hand, some may have no material possessions at all, but they are welcomed everywhere by others. So everything depends upon whether one has made affinity with others. The Buddha taught us that, "Before attaining Buddhahood, we need to make affinity with others." There are many ways to build affinity. Regarding others with a kind look is making affinity with our eyes; praising others with kind words is making affinity with our mouths. We can also make affinity with others through our service, skills, thoughts, and the Dharma.

"Affinity" is not a special Buddhist term, but rather the truth of life and the universe, and it belongs to every person. We all spend our lives in and around affinity. All opportunities represent affinity, and it takes the affinity of many for anything to succeed. In building a house, should there be a brick or a tile missing, the construction would not be complete. In the journey of life, some always come across help when they are in difficulty, and that is the result of having made affinity in the past. So the affinity made today will become the resources for resolving adversity in the future. "Making affinity" is therefore the best investment for future safeguard.

"Allowing others to take advantage" is also a way "to make affinity." Not only should we allow others to take advantage of us, we should also share whatever we have with others. That is because there is an interconnection between the self and other, and we are all combinations of causes and conditions. So in giving to others we are giving to ourselves at the same time, and in helping others we are also helping ourselves. Making affinity also helps resolve misunderstandings between people. If in ordinary times, we persist in making affinity by being tolerant and patient with others instead of holding grudges, then when the opportunity arises, others will certainly provide us with good causes and conditions in whatever we set out to do.

People rely on causes and conditions to survive in this world. The strength of the self is often insufficient, so it is necessary to make broad affinities everywhere, for the broader we reach, the greater our achievement will be. Sometimes a kind word, a kind deed, or even a smile may bring us broad affinity in life and help us to achieve great merit. Therefore, no one should give up any opportunity to make affinity. Making affinity broadens our life and clarifies our future; a life filled with merit and affinity is the true source of good fortune.

Duty and Responsibility

Once we are born, we all carry a duty to ourselves, our families, society, and our country—for life itself is a duty. Duty is benefiting others; it is the responsibility of the courageous and the ambition of the young and capable. If others give us a particular duty, then we should bravely take it on and be responsible for it. Those who have a sense of responsibility will only be concerned that the work is done and not care about success or failure, gain or loss. They will not bicker over how difficult the task is, but instead just put forth the best effort to accomplish their responsibility.

A sense of responsibility is the noblest sentiment in this world; those who act responsibly are capable of great achievements, while those who are irresponsible are actually inept, no matter how strong their abilities are. We should be responsible for whatever we choose to pursue because, as long as we are willing to bear responsibility, then there is nothing in this world that cannot be resolved.

Responsibility renders strength and confidence. If we are willing to bear responsibility, then there will be achievements. Not only should we be responsible for our duties, we should also be responsible for our mistakes. In order to progress and improve, we need to be responsible for and repentant of our mistakes. When we make mistakes, if we remain attached to what is wrong, blame others for our faults, or attempt to garnish support for our mistakes, we will never have hope for success.

In our learning process, we should not fear lack of recognition or the opportunity to test our skills. Instead, we should fear for the lack of courage to bear responsibility. How far we succeed in our careers is dependent on how much responsibility we can shoulder. Those with a sense of responsibility are able to overcome adversity and create good opportunities for themselves. But those who fear responsibility will end up complete failures, accomplishing nothing.

Life is an accumulation of experiences; therefore, it requires courage to take the first step in anything we do. If we are brave enough to bear responsibility, to accept the challenge, and to make the attempt, then there is nothing that we cannot achieve. Do not fear setbacks, for what is more important is whether we have the strength to shoulder responsibility. Strength comes from a tolerance for life and for all phenomena. Tolerance is the strength and wisdom we need to be responsible. We should be able to swallow our pride when required, be perfectly willing to hold the short end of the stick, and still remain self-assured. Then we will have achieved the open-mindedness that can embrace others and the universe.

It is a virtue to yield to modesty, but it should be based on reasoning. If we yield when we should not, we are acting irresponsibly. On the other hand, if we refuse to yield when we should, then we are too attached to our attributes. In handling affairs and dealing with others, we should be indifferent to fame and fortune, but serious about our duty. We need to cultivate the strength to bear responsibility, and we should start by getting to know ourselves and by training ourselves. We should not hide from our weaknesses or refuse to discuss them. To be able to face our shortcomings bravely and then to change them for good is to be truly responsible for the duty of self and life.

The Reality of Supernatural Powers

Life is filled with suffering and impermanence. When faced with difficulties or problems that cannot be resolved, many turn to the Buddhas, bodhisattvas, or deities for blessings. But often, under these circumstances, their greatest wish is to possess supernatural powers.

Supernatural powers are the incredible powers attained through the cultivation of concentration during meditation. These powers are extraordinary. They are completely carefree and unobstructed; therefore, the common man would like to possess these superhuman powers to realize every dream in life that would otherwise be impossible. However, could all wishes be fulfilled with supernatural powers? In reality, they cannot, for supernatural powers cannot override karma, because karma is the strongest power of all in this world. Also, supernatural powers cannot work against the principle of cause and effect. This is well illustrated by the Buddha's disciple, Maudgalyayana, who was foremost in his supernatural powers; but even with his powers he could not liberate his mother, who was suffering in hell.

Supernatural powers are not almighty, and possessing such powers actually can bring suffering. If you possess the power to know others' minds and discover the evil designs of your best friend, do you think you will have peace of mind? If you have celestial hearing and can hear one's close associate speaking badly of you, do you think you will be tolerant of one another? If you have the power to know about past and future lives and learn that you have only one more year left to live, do you think your life will be more at ease?

Furthermore, so-called supernatural powers are not the property of only Buddhas, bodhisattvas, deities, and ghosts, and such powers are not necessarily strange magical practices. Supernatural powers manifest themselves in many forms everywhere in the universe. Where dark clouds gather thickly, it will rain; or when air currents converge, there will be windstorms. The changing of seasons, the continuance of day and night, and all changes of natural phenomena can be considered forms of supernatural power.

Supernatural powers can also be witnessed in many ways in everyday life: water relieves thirst, food relieves hunger, those who swim well float in the water, and those who ride a bike go wherever they please. In addition, there are telephones, airplanes, and the Internet. They are comparable to celestial hearing, the power to transcend physical limitations, and celestial vision. Organ transplants and the cloning of animals are developments that were unheard of previously and are as sensational as any supernatural power.

Therefore, supernatural powers are the accumulation of human experience, the actualization of wisdom, and the highest utilization of capabilities. For with supernatural powers, there is the pursuit of form and existence, and with existence there are limits, quantity, and end; it is only with the empty nature of the truth that there are limitless uses. Supernatural powers are inferior to morals, and they cannot surpass emptiness. Possessing supernatural powers will not bring one happiness. Morals and ethics, on the other hand, are the real treasures that are inexhaustible. To be able to realize and understand the truth and its empty nature is the ultimate way to liberation.

Inspirations of the Moon

Once, a thief planned to sneak into a rich man's house to steal, and he brought his son along to learn the tricks of thievery. The thief told his son to keep watch for him outside the door and to let him know if someone came along. As he was about to practice his skills, his son suddenly shouted loudly, "Papa, someone saw us!"

On hearing this, the thief bolted quickly with his son and after running for a long distance, they stopped to catch their breath. "Who was watching us?" he asked his son.

The boy replied, "Papa, the moon was watching us!"

This tale teaches us that even if we think nobody knows that we do bad deeds, do we think heaven and earth do not know? Do we think bad deeds can escape the law of cause and effect and the Buddhas and bodhisattvas' knowledge? As the saying goes, "A sage will not fear the witness of ten pairs of eyes and the admonition of ten hands."

The moon has always been a subject of admiration for the kind and benevolent, lovers and poets alike. The bright shining moon high up in the sky has inspired many literari to compose and chant their sentiments. "How often can one appreciate the luminous moon and scattered stars?" This simple question illustrates that amidst remorse about life's brevity, there is the hidden sorrow and anguish of so many unfulfilled wishes! There were many people throughout history who endured grievances with no means of addressing them and bore suffering with no one to talk to. With nowhere to go, there was only the moon that would listen to them; theirs was

With the moon inside us, we need not fear the lack of brightness

indeed a melancholy lot!

Actually, the moon symbolizes brightness and wholeness. Lovers, bathed in the glow of their affection for each other, pledge their commitment, with the moon as their witness. However, life is filled with impermanence; even the moon is unable to control affairs. As the saying goes, "As the crescent moon shines on the great land, how many of its families are joyous and how many of them are sorrowful?" The moon waxes and wanes, shines and darkens, just as life is filled with sorrow and joy, gatherings and separations. From the moon's waxing and waning, we can fully appreciate the changing tides of life's happenings and our helplessness!

There is a verse that goes, "The ancients did not see today's moon, but today's moon once shone on the ancients." The moon remains the same throughout time; as it shone on the ancients, so it shines on us just as impartially. But while the ancient moon still exists today, the ancients are long gone! For those in the future, the moon that we see now will still shine on; but how is the future moon going to shine on us? The changing of time and the impermanence of people and things—no wonder poets are often stirred by the moon!

Another saying quipped, "The moon is especially bright at midautumn, but how many mid-autumns is one able to celebrate?" The moon may wane, but it will wax again; it may darken, but it will shine again. However, when life is over, when will it return? The ancients said, "The moon may wax and wane but it is always there. It actually does not darken, so why does it need to shine forth again?" To us the moon waxes and wanes, darkens and shines, but it is actually the result of the planet's revolution and dark clouds obstructing it from view. But the moon itself does not actually wax or wane, darken or shine; it is the same bright moon all along.

Regardless of whether it is waxing or waning, darkening or shining, the constant presence of the moon is beyond any doubt. So, as long as we have the sun and the moon in our minds, then "As the sun hangs high in the sky, and the bright moon shines in our hearts, with the sun and moon inside us, we need not fear the lack of brightness!"

Life is But a Traveler

Some say man is the master of the universe, but others believe that man is but a traveler. In the Chinese language, when judges go to court it is called "passing the hall," and in Buddhism, when monastics go for their meals in the dining hall, it is also called "passing the hall."

"Passing" means one cannot stay for long; it is a passing in a moment of time, just as our life in this world passes from birth to death, lasting only several decades. As we go through the process of birth, aging, sickness, and death, we arrive empty-handed and then leave in the same manner. Therefore, it is certainly appropriate to say that man is a traveler of the universe.

The universe is a journey for life, and life is its traveler. In going through the life of a traveler, some leave behind many records in the universe. There are loyal ministers and filial children, and also heroes and adventurers. Then there are malicious thugs and vicious bandits, and even notorious monsters. Some of them leave behind glorious colors while others bequeath a vile reputation to the world. There are some who portray heaven in the universe and still others who create hell in society. From history, we can judge from the actions of kings and emperors, scholars, and professionals, corrupt officials, and pirates of the high seas, the virtue and vice of their creations.

Because life is just a traveler of the world, naturally there are those who would like to leave a mark on history. Some would leave love and amity, others the sparkle of life. But there are others who come and go without a sound, not knowing why they come or why they leave. Just as people come and go in large hotels, they do not necessarily have a goal in mind. However, even when life is just a traveler of the universe, those who are able to manage time truly own life; and those who know how to make good use of time can handle life well.

Regrettably, among these same travelers of life, some cherish life and bemoan its brevity, but there are others who waste their lives away and complain about its lengthiness. In reality, if we truly knew life, we would realize there is much suffering in life. It is only when we are in control of our lives that we do not fear its pain and emptiness.

In traveling through the journey of life, some live life seriously while others simply follow their circumstances. Just as Chan Master Wumen said, "Spring has its blossoms and autumn its moon, summer has its breezes and winter its snow; if one has nothing to be concerned about, then any time is a good time in life." Whether it is spring or autumn, whether it is time for birth, aging, sickness, or death, the traveler of life comes quickly and goes just as quickly. We should therefore ask ourselves, "What is it that we can leave behind in this world that has a life beyond our own?"

The Almighty Human

Of all creations, humans are supreme. The human is also an almighty animal. For example, we have an almighty pair of hands that can do numerous things, a pair of feet that can take us anywhere in the world. Our eyes can see in different directions, and our ears can hear noises from all around. Our hearts and minds are better still, for be it heaven or earth, our imaginations can take us anywhere. All in all, it appears that God is not almighty; rather, it is humans who are so!

Of course, humans are almighty, but there are some who are incapable! When we speak about scholars, some may say, "Scholars are totally useless!" Some would even describe kings and emperors as "weak-willed and inept." Then there are others who fall on bad times and bemoan that they are incapable of anything. Some are incapable of answering their country's call to duty, others are incapable of serving their community, yet others are incapable of fulfilling their responsibility to their family, and still others are incapable of supporting their friends in their endeavors. All of those who do not shoulder any charges nor carry any burdens due to their perceived lack of capability are indeed pitiful. Actually, as humans, we are all capable!

There is this joke: "A drunkard was on his way home in the middle of the night, and passing by a graveyard, he accidentally fell into a grave that was dug for a funeral taking place the following day. No matter how hard he tried he could not get out, so he decided to sit and wait for dawn. At this time, another drunkard fell into the pit. He also tried to climb out of the grave with all his might, but failed at every attempt. Upon seeing this, the first man quipped, 'Hey! There is no way to get out, so don't waste your energy!' This unexpected voice that seemed to come from nowhere not only scared the second man out of his drunkenness, it enabled him to climb out of the pit!"

This joke illustrates that every one of us has unlimited potential, but everything depends on whether we know how to develop it and if we are willing to be an almighty person. If you look at someone who is capable, he should be able to get up early and stay up late, withstand cold or heat, go hungry or be full, be big or small, get up in front or stay behind, have more or have less, have or have not, be wealthy or poor, take honor or insult, and keep busy or take it easy; those who are truly capable can be anything. Therefore, people should have the conviction that humans are almighty. There are those who say God created man; we say man could create God instead.

In this world, all those who are capable can turn any crisis around and transform it into a matter of little or no consequence. They are able to simplify complicated affairs, transform selfishness into selflessness, and even "work miracles with junk." They are capable of creating the impossible, developing new technologies and new thinking, establishing successful careers, and even saving the world and its populace.

The Doors and Windows of the Mind

The doors and windows of the mind sometimes need to be open; at other times, they need to be closed. Similarly, physical doors and windows need to be open and closed at different times. We have to shut them tightly when thieves may be loitering outside the house or when the air outside is polluted. When we go to work, go out shopping, or when friends come visiting, if the doors of our offices, shops, or homes are not open, then how can communication in society or the family be smoothly accomplished?

Some do not know how to safeguard the doors of their senses, allowing all sorts of disruptive noises to enter through the cracks. These include improper language and unseemly gossip, which are like germs invading our domain and threatening the peace and harmony of the whole family. They are also like sand from a sandstorm, or polluted air wafting into the house through the open doors and windows, fouling the atmosphere and creating poor living conditions. The opening or closing of these windows and doors is indeed crucial!

However, when we do not need to shut the windows and doors of our houses, then they should be left open. If we have a happy occasion to celebrate, then we should open up our doors and tell all our friends and relatives about it. When there are gatherings in the house, then windows and doors must be open to welcome the visiting guests.

Venerable Master Hsing Yun built Fo Guang Shan, the biggest Buddhist monastery in Taiwan, to help people open the door of the mind

So, just as the doors and windows of our houses are our families' channels for communicating with the outside world, the doors and windows of our minds are key to the exchanges between our inner selves and the universe. Though the physical doors and windows may be shut tightly, the doors and windows of our minds still enable us to travel the world, although not in the same way as actually leaving and returning through the physical doors.

We should keep our doors locked and windows shut for safety reasons; however, we need to pay attention to their functions as well. When doors and windows need to be shut tightly, then we should do so, thus creating a safe haven for ourselves and our families. We need not fear the wind and rain outside, or the prying eyes of thieves, for when we have doors and windows, we are protected from their threats. But regrettably, some close off the doors and windows of their minds so that all good deeds and good people are unable to enter. Worse still, truth and sound reasoning cannot enter, and even righteousness and friendship are locked out. These kinds of doors and windows have become obstructions for the mind and not the channels that they should be.

Therefore, we should open up the doors and windows of our mind, so that "precepts, concentration, and wisdom" can enter as they should, and "greed, anger, and delusion" will go away as they should. Then, we will have achieved what is meant to be!

The Fruit of Diligence

Where there is hard work, nothing is impossible.

Where there is diligence, there are benefits.

Nothing is sweeter than the fruit of labor, but there will be no fruit if there is no labor. If we have a plot of fertile land, harvest will only be possible if we diligently till the earth and sow the seeds. These are the truths of everyday life.

If we refuse to see the truth in causation and insist on taking advantage of other's hard work, we will not only become a burden to society but will also bring harm to ourselves. Our lives will be in ruins forever because "being lazy" is the most unethical behavior a person can have.

In today's society, almost everyone wants to be rich. But we must realize that "being rich" has nothing to do with monetary or material possessions. We can have all the money in the world without "being rich," because in the blink of an eye, it could all disappear. For example, we may have a large inheritance, but without added income, it might dry up like a well. However, if we are willing to work hard, and to be diligent in whatever we do, we will be the wealthiest people in the world.

As long as we are diligent and willing to take initiative at work, our bosses will come to notice our progress, and our abilities will be of secondary importance. As long as we focus our attention on our efforts and try to be as diligent as possible, we no longer have to worry about what we can or cannot do. According to the Buddhist texts, "Indolence will cause laypeople to lose worldly benefits and monastics to lose the treasure of Dharma."

Although laziness is a vice and diligence a virtue, our labor and hard work must have positive meanings. They must be devoid of every selfish intention. In Buddhism, there are four kinds of "Right Effort": To produce and increase that which is good, and to prevent and eliminate that which is bad. By exerting our efforts for the purposes of benefiting others and guiding them toward goodness, we have not only reaped benefits for ourselves, but have also engaged in the correct practice of diligence. This kind of selfless act is the embodiment of the bodhisattva spirit. Therefore,

We have an abundant harvest, because we diligently till the earth and sow the seeds

if we want to see our efforts come to true fruition, we must learn to put the interests of others above our own and to sacrifice ourselves for the good of all. However, the habit of seeking pleasure and avoiding hard work is a social illness, for most people fail to realize that a moment of pleasure will produce a lifetime of misery, while a moment of diligence will result in an unexpected harvest. The underlying reason for this undeniable truth is that good causes will always bring about good results, and bad causes will always have retributions. This is the Law of Cause and Effect, the inescapable Truth of all universes.

The Tastes of Life

When we speak about the tastes of life, most would appreciate that they are sweet and sour, bitter and spicy. Some may say there are three different tastes in life. It is sweet when one is young; it is sour and spicy when one is mature and middle-aged; and then it becomes bitter when one is old.

Yet it is not always so! Many survive an unfortunate youth, such as being orphans, or homeless children and teenagers. They lost their homes, had nowhere to go, and no school would take them in. Not only did they not feel any sweetness in life, they were stung by the devastating, icy wind and bitter rain of life from a young age. When one is mature and striving for success in one's career, though there are the sour and spicy tastes of hard work, there are also the sweet tastes of achievement. Just as some purposely add vinegar or chili to their food, and the spicier it gets the more they savor it, so sour and spicy tastes are also needed for mature life.

As for bitterness in old age, it is due to the lack of achievements in one's life, especially when one fails to make broad affinities with others, and as the colors and luster of life fade with age, it will surely be bitter then. However, there are many seniors whose accomplishments go down in the history books and are lauded by others, or there are some who are known for their high morals and are respected by people in the community. There are still others who live a placid life, never at odds with anyone, and their serene retirement at old age is admired by many. The lives of all of these successful seniors are not entirely bitter.

In the past, some have often moaned, "If one does not work hard when one is young, then one will be sorrowful when one is old." Nowadays we should advocate, "One ought to work hard when one is young, then one will be full of joy when one is old." Life is filled with a hundred different kinds of tastes. So one should be like a chef in the kitchen, where the food of life is flavored. Be it salty or bland, sour or sweet, bitter or spicy—as long as it tastes good to the individual, then it should be so seasoned.

We should not complain about the various tastes of life. Provided that we have the appreciation and support of others, even if life is bitter or sweet, sour or spicy, there is nothing to be concerned about. The most important thing to remember is that we should selflessly offer others the real tastes of life: the taste of happiness, the taste of harmony, the taste of kindness, and any other tastes for that matter, as long as they are enjoyable. We should therefore offer everyone around us the very best tastes of life, and also adorn ourselves with them as well.

The sourness of pineapples can be turned into sweetness with sunshine and warm breezes

To Be One's Own Boss

A general may command a million brave soldiers in battle, but he may not be able to deal with his own wife at home. One may lead a crowd of people, but oftentimes may be unable to control his own worries. It is easy to be the head of a household, or the mayor, or even the ruler of a country, but it is very difficult to be one's own boss. For instance, can one control one's worries when one is sick? Can one control one's own death?

In your lifetime, have you ever thought about how to manage your time and be your own boss? How much time do you allocate for studying, working, and dedicating yourself to serving others? Or even for traveling and visiting abroad, meditating, and cultivating? Have you thought about how to manage your space and fully utilize the space in your home: its bedrooms, living room, study, and garden? Do you make full use of your office, and even public places such as parks, theaters, and department stores, in order to further expand the scope of your life? Have you thought of how to properly budget your money? Have you allocated the appropriate amounts for living expenses, donations, savings, and for your children's education? Have you planned in such a way that you have no worries? Some may, out of greed, lend money at high interest rates. But when the usurer goes bankrupt, then all of the money is lost. This shows he does not know how to manage his own money.

If you want to be a good head of the household, you must be able to benefit your family members. You will need to educate them and take care of their basic needs as well as their travel expenditures and medical costs. For if you cannot solve their problems, how can you be their "boss"? By the same token, if you cannot take good care of yourself, how can you be your own boss? If you want to be your own boss, you must develop a strong sense of awareness, enhance your abilities, and have a well-thought out plan for the future.

In reality, it is extremely hard to be one's own boss because one cannot control what the eyes want to see, what the ears want to hear, nor what the mind wants to think. Therefore, if you want to be your own boss, you should have your own opinion, and keep Chan, wisdom, and the

Buddha in your mind. Equipped with these causes and conditions, when you also apply perseverance and determination, you may one day be able to be your own boss!

Everyone holds a colorful pen to draw one's ideal of life

To Make Friends with Enemies

In society, we have friends as well as enemies. Enemies are not only those we confront on the battlefield where both sides set out to destroy one another. There are enemies in business, adversaries in the same occupation, and also opponents among those sharing similar advantages. As the saying goes, "Professionals are jealous of each other, and scholars are contemptuous of one another."

In dealing with enemies, the supreme strategy is not to destroy them. Rather, it is to subdue them without any actual fighting. Even in handling vicious and stubborn enemies, if we can win them over, and they are able to acknowledge their mistakes, then we need not destroy them. There are numerous incidents in Chinese history where those in power subdued their enemies with forgiveness, making friends with them in the end. Not only were the fighting parties spared animosity and sometimes bloodshed, the resulting peace and harmony actually enhanced the unity of the country.

In addition to not destroying their enemies, those who were capable would even assist them in becoming partners in growth and development. In Britain, the Conservative Party feared the loss of the balancing function of the opposing Labor Party; yet if the Labor Party came to power, they would also miss the interaction created by the Tories. So, they each supported one another in different ways to ensure that there would be an opposing party for competition. Francis Bacon, the British philosopher, once said, "One is lonely without lovers, and one is also lonely without enemies." This is so true. People become enemies for a number of reasons: due to a feud between families, war between countries, conflicts of interest, differences in ideology, or just being angry over some sort of injustice. Even friends may sometimes turn into enemies because of a misunderstanding, or one may have hurt the feelings of the other; or if one is being taken advantage of, then good friends may become sworn enemies.

Christians often say, "Love your enemies." Buddhism teaches, "Equality among enemies and loved ones." In reality, the greatest enemy in life is the self. It follows then that sickness is also our enemy and so is worry. Even though sickness is an enemy, we need to cure it or even be friends with it. Worry is our enemy, but we still have to face it and endeavor to "convert worry into bodhi."

Having enemies reminds us to be cautious, to take preventative measures, and to be diligent, for without them we relax and let our guard down. There were many ancient cavaliers highly skillful in martial arts who lamented for the lack of an opponent. Even on the basketball court, the two contesting teams thank each other, for without the other team it would be impossible for the game to take place. In the boxing ring, the opponents greet each other with courtesy, and after the fight the winner and the loser shake hands. After any election, the winners call the defeated opponents to thank them. Therefore, to be a friend or an enemy is only due to differences in position; it does not mean destroying each other.

In diplomacy, there is a saying, "Internationally, there are no permanent friends nor are there permanent enemies." Between people, sometimes friends become enemies, and sometimes enemies turn into friends. It all depends on how we treat others and what our views are. However, friends should remain as friends over time, but we should not let enemies remain enemies forever. Those who make friends with enemies are the truly capable ones in society.

To Never Retire

No matter where we live in this world or whom we work for, be it public service or private enterprise, there are retirement systems. Because of the several decades of life we dedicate to work, day in and day out, it is only reasonable that by the time we reach old age, we should be given the opportunity to rest and enjoy life.

Developed countries are glad to contribute toward government pension plans for those who have jobs so that they can receive retirement benefits when they retire. Throughout history, the Chinese also "saved up grain as a safeguard for a rainy day" and "raised children as a safeguard for old age." These are all measures for resolving the problems of retirement. Most countries have established the retirement age at sixty, sixty-five, or even seventy years old. As the saying goes, "The waves of the Yangtze River roll over one after the next." There should be plans in life for passing on the baton, as in Buddhism, there is "handing down the light," all of which are ways to deal with the changing of age and time.

When faced with retirement, for many, life suddenly seems empty and lonely, as if all is lost. With nothing much to do, their days are filled with boredom. This kind of retirement is like waiting for the arrival of death, for life has lost its meaning and sparkle. So, some are calling for "retiring but not resting." Actually, "as the heavens are progressing, the wise should be diligent in their self-improvement." In nature, the seasons change over time, and the constellations revolve unceasingly. As a part of nature, we should also recognize the imperative of "to be a monastic for a day is to ring the bell for a day," for life's meaning lies in enhancing the continuity of life in the universe. Therefore, we should not allow even a day in life to go by empty, for "even the morning dew may dissipate easily but it moistens the earth, and the winter sun may be short-lived but it melts the ice and frost."

The ancients were diligent in their resolve and practice, and did not carelessly waste any time, always persisting until the very end. Venerable Master Daoan passed away in the course of speaking the Dharma, and Venerable Master Huiyuan did so in the midst of chanting the Buddha's

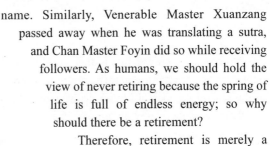

name. Similarly, Venerable Master Xuanzang passed away when he was translating a sutra, and Chan Master Foyin did so while receiving followers. As humans, we should hold the view of never retiring because the spring of life is full of endless energy; so why should there be a retirement?

Therefore, retirement is merely a change of jobs. We see how the youth study and learn, young adults establish their careers, and seniors pass on their experiences. We should retire without resting and continue to shine forth and blaze on in life. Be it Confucius in China, Jesus of the West, or Sakyamuni Buddha from India, they all have "worked" for over two thousand years. In people's minds, have they yet

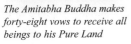

The Amitabha Buddha makes forty-eight vows to receive all beings to his Pure Land

retired? As the saying goes, "the silkworm only exhausts its silk upon death and the candle only dries its wax upon extinguishing." We should sing the praises of the greatness of life, for life never retires!

To Take Care of Our Thoughts

Life as a human is really not easy, for in addition to taking care of oneself one also needs to take care of family, friends, and society. Therefore, in the vastness of humanity, when one has to look after so many people and affairs, it seems that each and every human being is indeed a great person.

Look at taxi drivers. They work very hard driving from morning till night, making a living in order to raise a family. A street vendor gets up early to do business, providing breakfast for others, and in the course of his labor, makes a small profit with which he can support his family. Police officers patrol the streets to ensure that law and order in the community are protected, while those in civil service are busy with their work serving the country better. However, it is more difficult to take care of thoughts within the mind than matters of the external world.

Why is it so hard to take care of our thoughts? It is because our thoughts are in heaven this moment and in hell the next. Our thoughts not only travel all around the world all day long, they also go through transmigration in the six realms of existence at the same time. There is a saying: "There are thieves outside the doors of the six sensory-organs (e.g.: the eyes, ears, nose, tongue, body, and mind), wandering around day and night. When we go out in the streets without any purpose, to whom can we turn to when we run into trouble?" If we do not take good care of our thoughts, one deviant thought could leave us mired in trouble, just like the saying, "If we take one wrong step, we will regret it forever."

Do not think that thoughts have no shape or appearance, or that they are not realized in any form. Actually, what we think will be reflected in our appearance, and what we show on the outside comes from the inside. As the saying goes, "The three realms are of the mind, and all phenomena come from the consciousness." When our thoughts move, even the mountains and rivers move with them.

The force of nature is very powerful; for example, earthquakes and hurricanes are terrifying phenomena. But the power of a thought can be even more frightening. There is a saying, "When a thought of anger arises, a million obstacles will surface." When we are angry, we may even have the vicious impulse to kill. But if we have bodhicitta arising, then even our teacher may turn around and become our disciple. Therefore, if we have the right thought, even ghosts or deities may pay us homage. Conversely, if we have a deviant thought, they may decide to punish us for it instead.

There is a Chan saying, "If we can concentrate without wavering, there is nothing that we cannot accomplish." If our thoughts were calmed, then the universe would be luminous, for thoughts are like a lake. If the surface is smooth and quiet, then everything is reflected clearly. But if our thoughts become turbulent, then naturally we will be unable to see our true nature clearly. Therefore, we should always hold and maintain right thoughts in order "to cultivate any goodness that we do not yet possess and develop whatever goodness we already have; prevent any evil from developing and cease whatever evil we may already possess." If we are able to take good care of our thoughts, then even though we may not attain Buddhahood, at least we will be closer to becoming saints and sages!

To Walk Out of the Shadow

"While walking on a long and pitch-dark road in the middle of the night, along the way, every now and then, some unusual flashes appeared and strange noises sounded. Finally, there was light upfront, and thinking back on that dark and treacherous road one would still be filled with consternation." So wrote Dante in *The Divine Comedy*.

Those who have witnessed the devastation of war and its deaths and injuries, or have experienced the torture of kidnappers and robbers, carry with them dark shadows of life, which are difficult to eradicate. Similarly, there are women who have been raped, or young children who have been traumatized by excessive threats. They all have dark shadows that are hard to erase. After a typhoon, flood, or thunderstorm, shadows of the dark nights of rain and wind will remain. Suppose an earthquake toppled mountains and cracked open the land, collapsed buildings, and separated families with death—these shadows of grief and pain would be almost impossible to wipe away from the heart.

How can one walk out of these dark shadows of pain? As mentioned earlier, the night traveler needs to look for a lamp quickly, for once there is light, the darkness will be erased. But what is the guiding light of life?

First, it is the strength of religion. When life is overcome by dark shadows, how is one going to move on? At that moment, one has completely lost one's direction, and the guiding light of religion is urgently needed. If one can enter into the realm of the Triple Gem—the Buddha, the Dharma, and the Sangha—then one will learn that for every phenomenon in this world, there are causes and conditions. Everything is a manifestation of causes, conditions, and karma, so one need not take everything to extremes. Therefore, even if the house has collapsed, material possessions are lost, or the lives of family members are sacrificed, as long as one's faith remains intact, then the future is still filled with hope.

Second, it is the light of wisdom. Wisdom facilitates the understanding of the truth. The world is actually "a fragile nation, and the four great elements are empty and painful." One must realize that the myriad phenomena in the universe are all impermanent. Everyone has parents and many have children, but when "impermanence" manifests itself, then loved ones separate like birds in the forests, each flying its own way at the sign of danger. It is only when one uses wisdom to contemplate and to let go, to understand the emptiness and pain of impermanence, to realize the arising and subsiding of conditions, and to be able to use the light of wisdom to break apart the dark shadows, that one can move on with courage.

Third, it is the reformation of one's views. The experience of a natural disaster or a man-made calamity is like an encounter with death. One may suddenly discover that life is an illusive dream, something easily shattered. At this time, one needs to summon up the courage to pick up the pieces and rebuild one's fragmented life and wrecked home. One must ponder the notion that if the bad does not go, then the good cannot begin, because impermanence can be destructive on the one hand and also hopeful and successful on the other. For if one does not establish a new point of view, then there will never be a new life.

Fourth, it is the fortification of one's spirit. In order to walk out of the dark shadows, one needs mental strength and reinforcement. As mentioned earlier, religion, wisdom, and views can all be used for spiritual fortification. Once the spirit is fortified, then one can easily leave the dark shadows of life behind and build a new life. All in all, the shadows of the material world are easy to pass through, but the shadows within the mind can only be wiped away by oneself. If one can "diligently clean and wipe often," then there is no need to fear that the mind will "accumulate dust all around."

How do I walk out of the dark shadows?

A Life of Being Front and Center

There is a type of person who enjoys always being at front and center stage; they like to sit at the head table for dinner, be in the center of pictures, and they like to be ahead of everyone, even when walking. There are probably people like that around all of us.

To be seated at the head of the table for a meal is an indication of one's status, but we need to ensure that our own cultivation is adequate to receive the deference of others. Taking the central position for a photo is permissible as long as others are respectful of us. As for walking ahead of everyone, then we have to be sure that others are willing to follow behind. Otherwise, we need to be cautious, for if we take our positions inappropriately, then we may find ourselves either to be "on pins and needles" or to have already been removed by others in their minds.

We should not take the central position when taking a picture for it means we are not humble enough or respectful of others, and we may then lose their support. When we walk proudly and high ahead of everyone else, paying little attention to our superiors and knowing little modesty in our triumphs, we may be unaware of the dangers and pitfalls up front! We often notice that before being seated for dinner, everyone is hesitant about taking the head seat. It is of course a display of humility, but many times it is also because we do not savor the loneliness of high positions. On the other hand, to be overly humble would appear hypocritical. We should therefore know when to move up and when to step back—to take the middle path is the right way.

A parent, leader, or head of state should naturally be seated in the center because they are deserving. But if our role is inappropriate, then by assertively taking the center position, we may not be able to shoulder the pressure of being the pillar of the establishment, for we may not be up to the task. Those walking at the front are always rulers, seniors, or honored guests. But if we were to take our place at the front when we should not, then others will leave us behind as soon as they have the chance to.

We should not be at front and center initially; instead, we should first start from the bottom and go to the top, from the side to the center, and then from the back to the front. Without a solid foundation at the bottom, we should not move up too high too quickly because it could be dangerous there. If we do not work from the sidelines first and instead step into the spotlight immediately, we may not have sufficient light and power. The resources at the back should first be well-stocked before beginning the gradual move to the front.

Chan Master Guishan was the patriarch of a Chan sect, but he always had the spirit to stay as low as the earth. He even vowed to be an old ox to serve others in his next life. He is an exemplar for us in that his example demonstrates that we need to cultivate endless merit through serving others before we can become a bodhisattva at the top. There are many successful entrepreneurs in society who started out as service agents or salespersons before they attained their current fortune. Therefore, be it in handling worldly affairs or building a career, we should start by staying behind the scenes, and work ourselves up to the front. When our efforts are recognized by others, and when the causes and conditions are right, then like "the dragon leaping up into heaven," we will find ourselves to be always given the front and center positions by those around us.

A Life of Gratitude and Grudges

Some ask, "What is the relationship between people?" The answer is, "It is simply a life of gratitude and grudges!" A family of blood relations can turn into enemies over personal advantages and the family fortune. The intricacies of their gratitude and grudges can be as complex as a soap opera. Theirs is indeed "a family of gratitude and grudges." Within an organization, workers share common ideals and goals. But in fighting over promotions and opportunities, they become shrewd and competitive with each other, thus turning themselves into "an organization of gratitude and grudges."

The residents of a country can come from the same region, school, profession, or ethnic background. Yet some choose to attack or even kill each other. Amidst their constant fighting, they make themselves "a nation of gratitude and grudges." Countries throughout the world should be able to coexist in peace, help one another in times of trouble, and be friends with each other at all times. But hundreds of thousands died in World War I, and millions died in World War II. And there may be a World War III, or even a World War IV. We are living in "a world of gratitude and grudges!"

Reflecting on Chinese history and its dynasties, one will observe that violent discord as a result of hatred was not uncommon. Or, even when gratitude should have been repaid with kindness, it was repaid with battle and war instead. In the course of their never-ending fighting, friends became enemies, and vice versa. Consequently, there was no truth, no reasoning, and no trust between them. The history books are filled with nothing but page after page of gratitude, grievances, and grudges.

Actually, the gratitude and grudges of life need not be so clearly defined. In defining such, we should ask ourselves, "Will this distinction bring us success?" A Chinese scholar once said, "We should not forget those who benefited us and should know those who bear a grudge against us!" Therefore, we need to resolve all grudges.

The Buddha teaches, "To cease hatred with hatred is like trying to cool off a boiling pot by simply stirring it." But if we resolve a grudge with benevolence, then there is nothing that we cannot accomplish. A Chinese classic, *The Book of Odes*, states, "One should return a plum when given a peach." We should have the virtue of "repaying a drop of kindness with a gushing torrent of gratitude." In dealing with others, we have to learn to forget old grudges. By not carrying over any grievances to the next day, there is nothing that we cannot resolve in our so-called "life of gratitude and grudges."

The relationships between people are comprised of gratitude and grudges

A Matter of Course

In worldly affairs, be it between right or wrong, good or bad, some situations are a matter of course and others are not. For those that are a matter of course, we do not pay too much attention to them, but for those that are not, we reject them or grumble about them. As a result, we are ill at ease. When we are faced with prosperity, we may take it as a matter of course. So, in facing setbacks, we should also consider them to be a matter of course because "taking adversity with peace" will bring us much joy.

In nature, warm breezes can foster the growth and development of all living things. Similarly, frost and snow can also help them mature and ripen. In the journey of life, our parents may be strict with us so that we can grow up to be somebody; our teachers may push us to work hard so that we can achieve good grades. These are all a matter of course. Between classmates, there will of course be competition, for when there is competition there is progress. When others are cool and aloof, it is also a matter of course, for then we will be able to actualize life to its fullest. The Spartan training of armed forces is a matter of course, for the battlefield allows no mistakes. When the boss requires his workers to work overtime, it is also a matter of course, for profit is only possible with increased production.

It is a matter of course that children require their parents to nurture and educate them, because that is the responsibility of parents. When poor friends ask for a monetary loan, it is also a matter of course, because they need help in their situation. If we take all that is not a matter of course to be so, then we will have peace of mind and will not complain, just as it is a matter of course that flowers bloom in spring, the weather gets warm in summer, the land grays in fall, and the world appears lifeless in winter.

Others' wealth may be due to their hard work. That is a matter of course. Or, when others are prosperous, it may be because of their merit and good causes and conditions. The neighbors next door are harmonious and at ease because they are well-educated and cultivated. Or, if someone is doing well in their career, it is also a matter of course, for they have excellent qualifications and good fortune!

When we talk about suffering, we should take it as a matter of course; without the bone-chilling cold of winter, the plum blossoms would not be profuse in fragrance. We should therefore consider taking the short end of the stick as a matter of course. Within "a matter of course," there is so much merit and accomplishment! In the course of life, as long as we strive hard, taking everything as a matter of course, then there is no problem that cannot be resolved.

It is a matter of course that flowers bloom in the spring

A Sense of Danger

Education plays a very important role in today's world. We witness so many parents making all sorts of sacrifices and enduring different hardships, even migrating to other regions in order to provide the appropriate environment for their children's education. Nowadays, education in the family, school, and even in society is common and broad. However, what we lack is education on how to have a sense of danger. To have a sense of danger is to know about "prevention," such as how to prevent or cope with disasters, theft, fire, earthquakes, and fraud.

In today's life, we should always be on the alert and be prepared. When we go out we have to prepare for traffic jams, and when we drive we have to watch out for reckless motorists, should they run a red light and hit us. When women go out at night, they should be wary of stalkers, and every time we leave the house we should let our family know where we are going, so that they will know where to find us in case we go missing.

At home, we should guard our home's safety and be on the watch for our neighborhood, especially around holidays, for any possible burglars. We have to take measures such as not allowing any strangers into the house and not answering any unsolicited calls. We also have to check for unattended candles or fires, gas leaks, and improper wiring. In addition, other measures, such as stocking up on first aid materials, buying a flashlight and fire extinguisher, as well as getting a sufficient supply of non-perishable food, water, and cash are imperative for any emergency situation.

We need to be aware of current affairs in the world and the nation. We have to take appropriate actions during any economic downturn, inflation, or even unemployment. We also have to prevent political persecution and the false accusations of others. When we are lucky enough to win the lottery, we have to safeguard our fortune against thieves and robbers; and when we earn a promotion, we have to be aware of others' envy.

A couple needs to be wary of a possible third party coming between them; parents are to guard against their children's falling in with the wrong friends or picking up bad habits. In constructing a building, there are preventative measures that can be taken to help withstand the effects of earthquakes and hurricanes, and provisions should be made for emergency escapes and fire lanes. Between people, we all need to guard against fraud from strangers, friends, coworkers, or even family members. The best way to guard against fraud, of course, is to have no greed. Furthermore, whenever we have to stay in a hotel for the night, we should know the emergency exits, and when we eat out we should watch for cleanliness.

As the saying goes, "The winds and clouds of the heavens may change without notice, just as the fortunes of humans will vary at any time." We should be positive and constructive in life and be optimistic and joyful in our outlook, having faith in life's hope, beauty, success, and brightness. At the same time, we should also have a sense of danger by being alert and taking preventive steps to guard against any crisis we may face. To be prepared in times of crisis is positive at all times.

About Taking Forty Winks

Sleep is "nourishment" for our eyes, and an appropriate amount of sleep is necessary for us to move on further down the road. However, too much sleep is wasteful. Everyone has had the experience of dozing off due to insufficient sleep. Students may doze off in class, those attending a meeting may doze off in the middle of discussions, those working in their offices may doze off at their desks, and even drivers may doze off while negotiating dangerous terrain. No wonder even presidents will take forty winks in the midst of their hectic schedules, because when the sleep bug bites, there is no way one can resist! Some know how to doze well, while others do not; those who know how to do it well do not let others know they are dozing, but for those who do not, their sleepy ways can be really funny.

Some of them will support their heads with their hands like pretty women striking a pose; some throw their heads back as if calling upon heaven; others keep nodding their heads like little chicks pecking for food; still others waver left and right as if reciting a poem. Then there are those who snore loudly, and their thundering noise disturbs everyone around them. These are the ones who do not know how to take forty winks well.

Confucius did not like to see others dozing off. So when one of his disciples dozed off in the middle of his class and even started to snore rhythmically, he admonished him in front of everyone, saying, "Such rotten wood cannot be sculpted, just as a wall of mud and dung cannot be plastered."

Similarly, the Buddha did not like his disciples to take naps. He chided Aniruddha, one of his disciples, for dozing off, "You foolish man who enjoys sleeping, you would sleep for a thousand years inside the shells of conch, mollusk, and clam, unable to hear the name of the Buddha."

One time, in the middle of a Dharma function, some elder monks dozed off from fatigue while the young novice monks sitting at the back were attentive and poised in their seats. Upon seeing this, the Buddha asked, "What is the meaning of an elder?" He further explained, "An elder is not based on age; some may have been a monastic for thirty years but have spent those years sleeping. Conversely, there are those who have only been a monastic for three years and have cultivated diligently in those three years; the latter are the true elders."

People nowadays live very busy lives, and they become overly tired. Therefore, they are prone to dozing off. In order to prevent dozing off in public when the sleep bug bites, some rub menthol on their noses or support themselves with pens; others bite their tongues or pinch their thighs; still others simply stand up from their seats. All of these examples illustrate how difficult it is to overcome sleepiness. The president of a country usually has a heavy workload and a busy schedule. Therefore, it is understandable that he/she becomes physically tired and may doze off involuntarily. But for those who doze off whenever they attend a gathering or proceed to study, it is a form of slothfulness as well as a kind of sickness.

Buddhism teaches us to cultivate according to the middle path and not to go overboard in our practice. It is like playing a string instrument. When the string is tuned too tightly, it breaks easily; but when it is too loose, it cannot be played. Therefore, for those who have a busy workload and those who tend to doze off, they should decide for themselves the appropriate path between work and sleep, between keeping busy and taking it easy.

Accepting Hardship and Blame

We all need to work in order to live, and in the course of doing so, we need to be capable and wise. However, what we need most is to be able to accept hardship and blame. Most people can take hardship, but to be able to take blame as well is both difficult and invaluable.

Some are able to work very hard from the crack of dawn until late at night, withstanding cold and hunger and never complaining about it. In order to finish their work, they will take all sorts of hardships and risks, make all kinds of sacrifices, and even neglect nourishment and rest. They will not give their plight a second thought but are only bent on getting their job done with whatever it takes.

A homemaker will cook and wash, clean and scrub in her home. When it comes to bringing up her children, she is willing to help and guide them through thick and thin, giving up her lifetime in exchange for the happiness of her family. A loyal subordinate will follow his superior by looking after all sorts of details day and night, overcoming different kinds of obstacles in the course of his duty. A farmer will bear the heat of the hot sun or the battering of the wind and rain in order to cultivate his land. He does not fear suffering and never complains. A good harvest is the only thing that matters to him.

However, even while being able to take hardships, many will find it difficult to accept blame which is easy to come by because, regardless of the kind of work one does, it is impossible to please everyone. For instance, after working very hard all day, the boss may still blame his workers for not working overtime at night. Or even though product quality may have already been improved, the boss may still complain about the lack of progress.

In an organization, the learned ones may be considered incapable, the capable ones may be said to be inarticulate, then the articulate ones are criticized for not being multilingual, those who can speak a few languages are judged as being too aloof, and those who are warm and amiable are put down as being unattractive. All in all, people may be perfectly willing to put up with hardships, but once the blame begins, nobody is willing to carry on. Therefore, for those who willingly accept hardships and difficulties, words of comfort and kindness are often better than an increase in pay or a promotion.

A Buddhist sutra states, "Those who cannot accept slander, criticism, and scolding as the drink of sweet dew are not deemed to be great!" In our life and our work, it is impossible to be entirely blameless. But as long as we have a clear conscience, we do not have to please everyone. So, for those who are only able to accept hardships in their work, it is not enough, because to be able to accept blame as well constitutes real strength.

Chan Master Hanshan asked Chan Master Shide, "If someone defiles, bullies, insults, slights, despises, torments, and deceives me, what should I do?"

The latter replied, "Just bear with him, let him be, avoid him, tolerate him, respect him, ignore him, and see what happens to him a few years later!"

Indeed, this dialogue between the two masters provides us with encouragement.

Contemplation

"Contemplation" is a very important practice in Buddhism. It will bring unlimited benefit to our lives, regardless of our profession or social stature. But what is the objective of contemplation?

1. We must carefully examine our relationship with our fellow human beings to see if we have brought harm to them.
2. We must carefully examine the way we treat our material possessions to see if we have been wasteful.
3. We must carefully examine the way we accumulate our wealth to see if we have engaged in any unlawful acts.
4. We must carefully examine our love for others to see if we have indulged in any irrational behavior.
5. We must carefully examine our relationship with society to see if we have interacted improperly therewith.
6. We must carefully examine our minds to see if we have achieved the state of mental purity.

Very often, people have the tendency to neglect the "self" and to concentrate their minds on others' faults. Very often people have a tendency to judge a book by its cover and overlook its contents. Without proper contemplation of the self and others, we will lose sight of the truth and be troubled by worries. If we want to understand our relationship with the society that we are a part of and we want to achieve mental soundness, we must actively engage ourselves in reflection and introspection.

The *Heart Sutra* says, "Avalokitesvara Bodhisattva was moving freely in the deep course of wisdom when he beheld

To have contemplation is to have harmony

the five aggregates, and saw that in their own being, they were empty." Only when we arrive at an understanding of "contemplation" can we become a bodhisattva of true "freeness." Only when we have gained insight into the true nature of the five aggregates can we overcome all suffering.

The *Sutra of Contemplation of Amatiyus*, also called the *Sutra of Sixteen Contemplations*, teaches different kinds of contemplations. Similarly, if we can behold in our mind the moon, the sun, the water and the earth, we will be one with nature. If we can contemplate the true nature of all existence, our minds will be one with all phenomena. With such insight, we will rid ourselves of all miseries and receive infinite joy.

When the Buddha taught, he would first seek to understand the temperament of his listener. When a doctor treats a patient, he will first diagnose the nature of the illness. When a farmer plants the seeds of next season's harvest, he first observes the weather pattern. When a parent asks a child to complete a task, he will know firsthand the limitations of his offspring. Therefore, to have success in our undertakings, we must have proper understanding and observation.

To have contemplation is to have harmony. To have contemplation is to have support and relevance. To have contemplation is to have satisfaction and pleasantness. To have contemplation is to set foot on the path of enlightenment. For a businessman, "contemplation" means market research. For a developer, "contemplation" means land survey. For a politician, "contemplation" means a thorough understanding of peoples' problems and needs.

If a person knows how to contemplate, he will have insight into the relationship of cause and effect. If a person is willing to contemplate, he will have a firm grasp on the true nature of existence. A practitioner of Buddhist meditation has the ability to rediscover his Buddha Nature through introspection. He has the ability to calm his mind through insightful contemplation. Once the dust has been wiped off and the Buddha Nature resurfaces, there is no doubt in one's mind that life will be complete. There will be absolute completeness, with nothing to add or subtract.

Correcting One's Shortcomings

"To err is human." Faults are our shortcomings. As the saying goes, "The greatest virtue is to be able to correct our mistakes."

Our parents have been correcting our shortcomings since we were young. We were taught to be tidy, to hold our chopsticks correctly, and to get up promptly in the morning. Do not overeat, do not tell lies, do not be naughty, etc. Similarly, our teachers in school told us to speak gently, to walk properly, and not to fight or make trouble. At work, our superiors also correct our faults, be it to write better memos, to speak better to customers, to deal more effectively with different levels of coworkers, or to handle affairs better. All in all, the foundation of life lies in correcting our shortcomings.

Benjamin Franklin indicated that he spent his lifetime correcting his faults and improving policies for the country. In his youth, he was considered an unruly person. He was awakened to this reality one day and realized that such a person would never succeed in life. So he decided to eradicate all the flaws in his character. He proceeded to list all his bad habits and undesirable traits on the wall. For instance, he wrote that he was argumentative, impolite, tardy, impatient, stubborn, selfish, lazy, disrespectful, intolerant, calculating, etc. He vowed to correct all of these shortcomings. Every day, he reviewed his behavior and speech and compared them with the writings on the wall. Once he found them corrected, he would erase those particular faults off the wall. After a long period of time, he corrected his mistakes and succeeded in cultivating an amiable and likable personality. He was loved by the masses and eventually became a senior statesman in the United States of America.

In dealing with others and handling our affairs, if we often blame others, we should realize that the problem might actually lie with us. If we are intelligent enough, we should reflect on ourselves. We should blame ourselves the way we blame others, and forgive others the way we forgive ourselves. Someone who knows how to reflect on himself will surely be welcomed by all.

There is a saying, "It is easier to move mountains than to change one's character." However, if something is difficult, it does not mean it is impossible. If we have the resolution and courage to change, even though it may be difficult at first, no bad habits are impossible to correct. We should be brave in our resolve to correct our shortcomings; then we may eventually become a perfect person who is respected by all.

It takes time to correct our shortcomings

The Empty Nest

In agricultural society, it was not unusual to have a large and close-knit family. Children usually stayed home to help their parents with field-work. Even when they grew up and got married, to maintain a strong network of support, they would not move too far away. The parents were never alone, even in old age, for there were numerous grandchildren as their companions. There was no such thing as the "empty nest syndrome."

However, with the passing of time and the arrival of the Industrial Age, our society has undergone a tremendous transformation. More and more people have moved into the city, making it more and more crowded. With limited living space available, parents have chosen to have fewer and fewer children. Today, a typical nuclear family consists of a mother, father, two children, and maybe a dog.

As children grow older and move away from home, parents are left with an empty house and sometimes a feeling of emptiness; their life is suddenly rendered meaningless and without a center. The empty nest syndrome is not unique in any way and is often a problem for today's parents. Children leave home like birds leaving the nest, in search of their own future. Feeling sad and perhaps abandoned, parents are now faced with the problem of starting their life anew. They must make a series of adjustments in order to avoid the bottomless pit of despair.

It is natural for parents to miss their children, but in reality, nothing in this world stays together forever. Life is full of comings and goings. There is no such thing as "we will be together eternally." There will always be departure. Therefore, parents must remain calm and composed when their young chicks are ready to fly the coop. They must not be overly anxious when their children are ready to say goodbye.

What should parents do to avoid overreacting? What steps should they take to minimize the devastating effects of the empty nest syndrome? Parents should first harvest broad affinity as much as possible. They should be virtuous and broadminded, for in this way, they will be parents to the entire world. Parents who are without virtue or who are unwilling to establish proper parent-child relationships will not be parents to their own offspring. They will be like strangers even to their own children.

As long as one understands the impermanent nature of the world and takes everything in stride, one will not suffer the negative effects of empty nest syndrome. Instead, one can use this opportunity to enrich one's own life. One can devote oneself to charity work and public service. One can take time out to enjoy life as it is and to broaden one's horizons. Therefore, having an empty nest can be a blessing in disguise. As for today's young parents, they should develop some kind of hobby, so they will not be miserable when their children are ready to live their own lives.

The following are a few suggestions on dealing with the empty nest syndrome:

1. When the nest is empty, we can invite our friends and family to our home to give it life.
2. When the nest is empty, we can learn to develop a reading habit because books can offer a wide range of experiences and a sense of peaceful abidance.
3. When the nest is empty, we can begin to cultivate new hobbies, such as gardening, to beautify our living environment.
4. When the nest is empty, we can extend our love to include strangers. We can do volunteer work at hospitals or schools. We can even go to a temple or church to enrich our spiritual life and to make friends.

When the nest is empty, we can devote ourselves to religion. We can replace family reunions with religious gatherings. As the *Vimalakirti Sutra* states, "The joy of the Dharma can be one's spouse, honesty and goodness can be one's children, the Four Meditative States can be one's bedpost, and liberation can be one's nutrient." As long as we are sincere and diligent in our pursuit of true enlightenment, our lives will not be empty, even if our nest is.

We can take time out to enjoy life as it is and to broaden our horizons

Encouragement Versus Criticism

To replace criticism with encouragement and to substitute insult with a word of praise is not only the best way to educate but also the best way to deal with others. In any relationship, conflicts are created for many reasons, but they are mostly due to excessive criticism and a lack of encouragement. This often results in subordinates leaving their jobs and friends becoming estranged, a major flaw in dealing with others and handling affairs.

Everyone has a pair of eyes, but they are all too often used to look at others' slip-ups, mistakes, faults, and shortcomings, instead of one's own problems. Everyone has a mouth, but again, it is only used to speak of others' flaws and weaknesses. Or, one may even purposely slander others and speak well of oneself. When we speak, our words are for others to listen to, and we just hear what we like to hear. Parents who overly criticize their children only see their children leaving them, and couples who overly blame each other end up with problems in their marriage. With friends, if finger pointing were the common practice, then it would be extremely difficult to maintain a lasting and trusting friendship.

However, this does not mean that criticism should not exist in a relationship. When the emperor criticizes, it is only a sage who can accept the criticism. Those who lack confidence must be given support and encouragement. A marathon runner needs much applause for that extra boost to finish the race. National awards, trophies, medals, scholarships, and all types of honors and tributes are for the encouragement and recognition of achievement. Even pets, such as cats and dogs, need to be praised, and cows and horses require encouragement from their owners. In order to flourish, plants and flowers need nourishment from the wind and rain. Those who have lost faith in themselves may blossom in their career upon hearing a kind word of encouragement from others.

In today's society, those with low social status are often criticized by their superiors. But in reality, those on top also frequently face criticism from the public because of their incompetence. There was a common saying in traditional Buddhist monasteries, "Even dogs would detest the supervising monastic who served for three years." Too much criticism can be demoralizing, and conversely, inappropriate encouragement can also be undesirable. Nevertheless, we should use a word of encouragement to replace criticism and a word of praise in place of insult; for after all, every person prefers encouragement and praise. So why should we be stingy in giving others praise and helping them on their path to success?

Exceeding Limits

Life is like the fingers of a hand: to be the thumb is to be number one and the best, to be the index finger is to command and lead, to be the middle finger is to be in the center and the longest, to be the ring finger is to be the bearer of diamonds and gold; and to be the little finger, is to be the one who needs to think, "Once in joining palms upon seeing a sage or superiors, I am closest to them."

It is human instinct to challenge limits. For instance, developers want to construct the tallest building, engineers wish to build the longest highway, and students want to get the highest grade. Everyone wants to create the next Guinness record. We all want to be world champions of some sort.

Emperor Qin built the Great Wall of China and won a name for himself by creating one of the wonders of the world. Alexander the Great wanted to conquer the whole world with his great ambition. Napoleon wanted to unify Europe so that his empire could continue from generation to generation.

Once the wish of every boxer in the world was to defeat Mohammed Ali. All marathon runners dream of being the world record holder. Track and field athletes all wish to run the fastest, jump the highest, and leap the farthest. This is because they all want to exceed life's limits in the world of sports. The richest man in the world builds various business empires in the pursuit of being the wealthiest, the most authoritative, and the most accomplished. The reason is that everyone aspires to exceed life's limits.

There are also individuals who have challenged the limits of life with many daring feats. The four-year-old girl who swam across the Yangtze River in China; the Singaporean man who leaped over the Yellow River Gorge with his motorbike; the daredevils who floated down Niagara Falls in a barrel; and the adventurer who traveled around the world in a helicopter. They all risked their lives so they could go down in history as being the foremost.

Every person possesses limitless potential and wishes for improvement. The pursuit of the best, the most beautiful, and the highest goal is the human instinct to excel beyond life's limits. However, there are many who are satisfied with what they have and others who simply compromise with reality and dare not challenge themselves to exceed their own limits. In reality, wisdom is the greatest limit in life, for it enables us "to understand causes and conditions and to be enlightened to the truth of life and death." Compassion is the greatest limit in life, for it enables us to "be compassionate to all beings." Generosity is the greatest limit in life for it enables us to "offer one's body to the ten directions." Attaining Buddhahood is the greatest limit in life for it enables us to "be liberated from life and death." In practicing the Dharma, we progress toward life's limits and take on the challenge of attaining Buddhahood.

The Great Wall of China was built by Emperor Qin

Faith is Treasure

Once upon a time, a philosopher was swimming in a lake when all of a sudden, a current pulled him under. As he frantically struggled to stay afloat, a thought entered his mind: "I am a philosopher, so I should not panic when faced with a life and death situation." When he began to relax his body and mind, the water's buoyancy pushed him to the surface and he was able to swim back to shore under his own power. This story shows that when one has faith in oneself, one will have infinite strength.

Faith and confidence are our inner treasures. If we have belief, we will have faith. If we have faith, we will have unlimited resources. The problem with today's society is that people have limited themselves by searching for resources from without. Even if there were an abundance of material supplies in our world, they would eventually run out. The energy shortage has become a crisis for many countries, which forces them to send experts into undeveloped areas in search of a solution. In actuality, we are all experts in excavating new resources, as long as we are able to look within instead of without. If we are willing to uncover our inner treasure, our lives will be enriched indefinitely by our faith.

To have faith is to have unwavering confidence. To have faith is to uphold and observe the truth. To have faith is to practice the teachings of the Buddha without doubt. By having faith, our body and mind will be purified. By having faith, we will have unlimited strength. In chanting the six-syllable dharani, "Om Mani Padme Hum," mispronunciation will not alter the effect of the dharani, if the chanter is sincere and focused. This is so because of the power that is inherent in the chanter's unquestionable faith.

In addition to confidence, credibility is a very important human characteristic. A person who is confident and credible will be successful in whatever he does. In order to eliminate conflict, contradiction, discrimination, and the illusion of gains and losses, one must have faith. The *Avatamsaka Sutra* says, "Faith is the foundation of the right path, the mother of all merit. It nourishes the root of all that is good." Without faith, one would not set foot on the path to enlightenment. By being skeptical and doubtful, one will not have a glimpse of the ultimate Truth.

Faith and confidence are our inner treasures

Faith is like a ray of light that will show us the way when we are lost in darkness. Faith is like sunshine that will brighten our day when we are feeling down and out. Faith will rekindle our hopes when we have failed miserably. *The Song of Faith* reminds us, "One should acquire worldly wealth with the hand of faith. One should cross the vast ocean with the boat of faith. One should grow plenty of fruit with the root of faith. One should receive unlimited treasure by entering the gate of faith. To have faith is to have hope; to have confidence is to have strength. Faith is the source of all virtues, the caregiver of wisdom. There is unlimited treasure in faith and confidence."

We are our own worst enemy. When we lack self-confidence, we are doomed to failure. However, if we have faith in ourselves, we will not only be successful in our worldly endeavors, we will also acquire the worldly karma necessary for enlightenment. Therefore, in this world, there is nothing more precious and valuable than faith and confidence.

Fame and Fortune

Every day, people commute in trains, buses, ferries, and airplanes, going about their business. Among them, some are on their way to serve others, and others are going to teach. There are those who are out there to benefit others. But most people are out there for their own fame and fortune.

There is nothing wrong with fame and nothing improper about fortune. With fame, we should pursue it and use it in a manner that is benevolent and positive. And with fortune, we should earn it through legal and benign means. However, it is not in our best interest, if, in the pursuit of fame, we achieve infamy. Or if, in going after profit, we create negative conditions for ourselves.

Many years ago, Fo Guang Shan hired an attendant, with a considerably high salary, to look after the public washrooms. However, whenever someone used the facilities, she asked them for a small tip of NT$2. The monastery made it clear to her several times that she should not do so because she was already paid for her work. But she said that if she did not get her tip of $2, just sitting there was too boring. She would rather quit her job. So the pursuit of fame or fortune is also a pastime for those who are bored.

Speaking of fame, there is a Chinese saying that goes, "A good name should be pursued for the first three generations in order to get established. It is a concern if the next three generations do not care for a good name in their enjoyment of the fruits of their ancestors." A truly good name should be sustained by morals, compassion, and generosity. If we serve the community and contribute to the well-being of humankind, others will sing our praises. But, unfortunately, most people in the world are bent on going after vanity. They are oblivious to the consequent notoriety they gain. This is truly unwise.

As for fortune, there is nothing amiss in seeking fortune with our capital, in sharing our fortune with others, or in making a profit for sustenance. If we pursue a profit deceitfully, or sacrifice morals for money and ruin our lives as a result, we are shortchanging ourselves!

The most precious thing in the world is not money or reputation. Nor is it personal fame and fortune. Good health, joy, contentment, and harmony are far more important. A renowned Chinese general once said, "When leaving his position, a loyal subject should not blame his lord or country for the sake of his reputation." The name of the country is far more important than that of the individual. We should place the reputation of our community, family, parents, teachers, friends, and peers above ours, because when everyone enjoys a good name, we benefit likewise.

If we truly know how to live, we should be like the floating clouds and flowing water. We should be free and at ease. We should not allow fame and fortune to bind us, set our limits, or foreclose on us, because the greater the craving for fame and fortune, the less "smile" we have. Likewise, the more fame and fortune we possess, the greater is the pressure on our lives. We should share our fame and fortune with our friends and family. We should benefit our communities and our country. With fame and fortune, we should aim to help humankind, so fame and fortune will not only last momentarily but endure through the ages. This is true fame and fortune.

We should not allow fame and fortune to bind us

Fast Food Culture

We live in an age of rapid developments in science and technology. Though people are actually miles apart, advancements in transportation and communication shorten the distance between them, and our world has become ever smaller. In such a compressed world, every second counts. As a result, all kinds of "fast food" have been invented that are now a large part of the contemporary diet.

The invention of "fast food" is highly advocated by modern people and many think that, for instance, a cup of instant noodles is an effortless, quick snack ready to eat in less than two minutes. But actually, hours or even days of human effort went into the process of making the instant noodles. Yet, when we are enjoying a convenient snack of instant noodles, do we ever think about the hard work that went into it? A hamburger costs about a dollar. Yet the causes and conditions that went into producing the hamburger also involved much sweat and toil. Though the hamburger only costs a dollar, its real worth to the consumer really depends on how he views it. Furthermore, should someone want a bowl of hot soup, it is easily available by simply opening a can or tearing off the aluminum foil and adding hot water. Such conveniences are not limited to food only. If you want to take a picture, there are disposable cameras. If you have a baby, disposable diapers are available. There is even disposable paper underwear.

With the development of this instant, disposable "fast food culture" the world has become "fast" as well. In the past, traveling between the continents required taking long rides aboard a ship, which lasted a few months or even a year. Today, you can get on a plane in the morning and arrive at your destination the same night. Sending a letter to someone also meant a lot because it took a few months to be delivered, giving rise to the Chinese saying "a letter is worth more than gold." Today, there is priority mail, express mail, and even next-day mail. Faster still, there are now telephones, faxes, and emails that can deliver messages instantly; we really do live in a global village. When a soccer game is televised from Europe, fans from all over the world can watch it from their own television sets, as if they were all there in the stadium. It seems as if there are no more boundaries of time and space in today's world. Thus, many are prompted to speak of three dimensions, or even five dimensions.

Since the old days, humans have always wanted everything to be fast and convenient. In the Buddha's time, King Prasenajit wanted his new-born princess to grow up instantly. We all know how foolish that was because nothing in the world could grow up or develop fully in an instant. While many live life with "fast food," to believe in the existence of a "fast-food life" is delusional. Life does not arise instantly.

In Buddhism, we speak of time in terms of the past, the present, and the future. With space, we speak in terms of here, there, and the limitless ten directions. When we speak of life, we talk about births from the womb, egg, water, and metamorphosis, which are also limitless. In reckoning time, no matter how fast, it can still be measured in the Buddhist measurement of a ksana, sixty-three of which are contained in a snap of the fingers.

In terms of space, light and electricity travel the fastest. Yet the human mind is faster still. A single thought is able to traverse the universe and the ten directions instantly. Humans have already landed on the moon, and in the future, we may be able to travel in space the way the mind can.

Therefore, everything in this ever-changing world is within the scope of Buddhism. No matter how "fast" and advanced everything gets, in contrast with limitless time and space, it is still no faster than one "ksana!"

Good Health and Longevity

Everyone wishes for good health and longevity. So what is being healthy? Anything that is right, complete, pure, and harmonious is healthy. It is easy to recognize physical health, but mental health is also important, and it can only be appreciated when we pay attention and reflect upon it.

Other than physical and mental health, there is also emotional health, career health, monetary health, as well as the health of relationships and of religious beliefs. Therefore, even if a person may possess mental health, without the others, life can still be considered incomplete and unhealthy.

And what is longevity? Longevity does not simply mean a life of eighty or a hundred years of age. The turtle and crane enjoy a long life, and some trees even live for a thousand years. What are the contributions of these long-lived animals and plants to the human world?

In addition to physical longevity, we also need longevity of education, work, reputation, ethics, wisdom, and harmony. If longevity is limited to the physical body, without the mental support of education, work, ethics, and wisdom, then a long life will be meaningless.

Those who enjoy a strong physique are sometimes derided as having an overdeveloped body with an underdeveloped mind. If that is truly the case, then what is the value of possessing such physical health? So to be healthy is to enjoy physical, mental, and spiritual health. If one lives one's life with physical health but without emotional health, one will not be able to live happily. Or, if one's beliefs are wrong, without spiritual health, one will also find life difficult.

The legendary Pengzu of ancient China was said to have lived eight hundred years, but there is little in history about his contribution to society. Therefore, real longevity means merit, morals, and education, just as Buddhism teaches; to have compassion, kindness, joy, and generosity is true longevity.

In the pursuit of good health, we should instead seek completeness, and in the quest for a long life, we should consider having limitless life.

This is because good health does not mean completeness; thugs and bandits may also enjoy good health, but are they complete people? Centenarians who let their days pass by without doing much; is their longevity contributing anything toward society? So, for those of us who pursue good health and longevity, it is necessary for us to be aware of their true meaning.

Habitual Tendencies and Habits

Every person has habitual tendencies and actions. While habitual tendencies are usually neutral, for example, one can enjoy eating, sleeping, shopping, or looking good; habits on the other hand, can be good or bad. For instance, being neat, poised, polite, and cheerful are good habits, while gambling, smoking, drinking, and being lazy are bad habits.

It is easier to change one's habits but more difficult to change or be rid of one's habitual tendencies. As long as one has determination, one can change one's bad habits and develop good ones. For instance, if one likes to gamble, one should stay away from gambling places; or if one likes to drink, then one should keep one's hands off of all alcohol. Eventually, all these bad habits can be transformed. However, habitual tendencies related to worry not only affect this present life, but may also affect future lives the way karma does. Mahakasyapa, a disciple of the Buddha, had already attained arhathood, but the moment he heard any music, he could not help himself and immediately began to dance. Even bodhisattvas who have attained the fifty-first stage of enlightenment, but still possess a small fraction of ignorance and habitual tendencies, are like the moon on the eve of a full moon, not quite complete.

There is a fable: Once, a scorpion wanted to cross the river, so he asked the tortoise to carry him over. But the tortoise feared the scorpion's poison, so the scorpion reassured him, "Don't worry, since you are carrying me, if I stung you and you died, I could not live either!"

The tortoise thought that was reasonable, so he carried the scorpion on his back and swam into the river. When they got to the middle, the scorpion stung the tortoise in the head. The tortoise was very upset at the scorpion for breaking his promise and stinging him. With much regret, the scorpion said, "I didn't mean to harm you, but I am used to stinging others, I'm really sorry!"

As the saying goes, "It is easy to cease worries but difficult to change habitual tendencies." So, how are we going to change our bad habits and develop good ones? Others can only help us in some ways. We need to apply effort and have the determination to do it ourselves. For example, suppose we have always been lazy; if we do not work hard to change ourselves, even with the best teachers and friends by our sides, they cannot help us in any substantial way. Or, if we are so avaricious that we steal and cheat to satisfy our greed, we will probably not awaken to our crimes until we are thrown in jail for them. Therefore, in order to change bad habits to good ones, other than the influence of our surroundings and the impact of education, the most important factor is our own determination.

So, should our action, speech, and mind be affected by bad habits, we need to have the willpower to cut them away. This can be likened to a rusting knife that needs to be sharpened quick and hard, or the splintering wood that needs strong reinforcement to regain the strength for proper use. Habits are hard to change; habitual tendencies are more difficult to correct. As the saying goes, "It is easy to move the rivers and mountains but hard to change one's nature." When our nature becomes tangled, the entanglements are habitual tendencies. Our nature is influenced by the world's ways and habits, so we need to expend great effort to purify ourselves. Just like an ancient mirror that is tarnished with dirt and dust, without constant scrubbing and cleaning, how can it possibly regain its clarity?

Honey on a Blade

There is a parable in Buddhism comparing life to a dry well. Once there was a traveler going about his way, when suddenly a tiger appeared and chased after him. As he was running from the tiger, he saw a dry well by the road and climbed into it, supporting himself with a vine hanging from a tree. After he calmed down, he took a look into the well and saw four large snakes at the bottom. Petrified, he dared not move and remained hanging in midair. Looking up, he found there were now two mice, one white and one black, gnawing at the vine he was hanging on. Gripped by fear, he did not know what to do next, with a tiger outside, poisonous snakes crawling down under, and the vine he was clinging to about to be gnawed through by the mice. Suddenly, five bees flew over his head and dropped five drops of honey right into his mouth. The traveler found the honey to be so sweet that he forgot about the imminent danger he was in.

What this parable teaches us is that we live in the dry well of life and death, chased by the vicious animal of impermanence. Clinging to the lifeline of our karma, we drop into the well where four poisonous snakes reside (symbolizing the four great elements of earth, water, fire, and wind), ready to tear us apart. Then, there are the two mice of night and day gnawing away at our lifeline. And then bees overhead offer us five drops of honey, enabling us to forget our danger for the time being. That is "honey on a blade," and because of the sweetness of the honey, we easily forget the danger of cutting our tongue on the blade—a mirror of life.

What is honey on a blade? It is the taste of money, sex, fame, food, and sleep, the "five pleasures." In our worldly lives, there are all kinds of suffering: the physical suffering of aging, sickness, and death, and the mental suffering of greed, anger, and delusion. There is also the suffering of love and hate, good and bad, right and wrong, and also of war and other disasters around the world. All of these are borne by humankind because of the temporary pleasures brought by the five drops of honey. We are perfectly willing to bear with suffering.

When we think about it, in the span of our short and illusive lives, "the sunset is beautiful, bringing us closer to night," meaning life is like "a fish with less and less water." What joy is there? However, in facing our valuable lives, we should not be defeated by suffering and impermanence. We should create endless enterprises and actualize the value of life during our limited lifespan. We should never be deluded by greed for the honey on the blade, thereby ignoring our life and death.

As the verse goes, "We should pick the flowers while they are in bloom and not wait for them to wither, leaving only an empty branch." This is the kind of positive attitude we should adopt about our limited lives! In the face of invaluable life, we should not be defeated by suffering and impermanence.

In the face of our invaluable life, we should not be defeated by suffering and impermanence

How to Settle Oneself

Groups of homeless people band together and protest at a government office, requesting housing; an incapable employee fired by his boss is anxious about where he will go next; a street drifter chased about by the police each day needs shelter; and those who, for whatever reasons, cannot return to their homes all suffer.

The basic necessities of life include food and a place to live. Some settle in elegant houses or grand mansions, but when these buildings collapse or burn down, what are they going to do? Others settle into their time listening to sounds: to broadcasts, music, people speaking, or even the chirping of birds and insects. But when the sounds are gone, how are they going to spend their time?

The *Diamond Sutra* teaches that one should not be attached to form, sound, smell, taste, touch, and phenomena—the six dusts. Then how should one settle oneself? Some pursue money every day, but wealth is impermanent, as it is controlled by the five external factors: thieves, fires, floods, rulers, and prodigal children. Money is like flowing water, coming and going incessantly, only providing anxiety between the gains and losses; it is not for anyone to settle into for life.

Some may like to settle into love, but love changes like the blowing winds and floating clouds. Most of the time, love cannot withstand the test of changing circumstances, resulting in numerous incidents of divorce, abandonment, and extramarital affairs. Some may choose to settle on their careers, rushing here and there, day in and out, rarely even having the time to go home for dinner, ending up with a broken family. Others may settle into their studies. While they may do very well, others may regard them as bookworms. Still others settle on religion, but if they choose the wrong belief and become too superstitious or involved in cults, then they are even worse off.

All of the above are usually considered viable alternatives to settle down into, but none of them are completely appropriate, and the inappropriate ones should not be considered at all! For when people settle on eating, drinking, and reveling, they end up without achievements; if they settle on gambling and carousing, they lose all they have. There are others who settle on the mountains and water, but these are part of nature and cannot be possessed privately. Still others may choose to settle on fame and fortune, but "fame is like a night's dream and fortune is fall's frost. These cannot be settled on for long.

So how should we settle ourselves? The *Avatamsaka Sutra* says, "To take joy in gentleness and tolerance, to settle on compassion, kindness, joy, and generosity." As we look for a place to settle our bodies and minds, if we enjoy gentleness and tolerance and have compassion, kindness, joy, and generosity, then we have found our place to settle down, for that will be our eternal home!

How should I settle myself?

In Our Own Hands

When dealing with our emotions, successes, and failures, or our lives in general, we as humans should handle these matters within the grasp of our own hands. We should act as our own masters. As the saying goes, "There is no natural born Sakyamuni, nor any such Maitreya." Everything depends on our own efforts. As long as we strive toward our goals, we will be rewarded accordingly.

Some people become distressed merely because of what others say and, as a result, have trouble eating; some become upset over some small matter and have trouble falling asleep. When others can control the ups and downs of our lives, so that we feel happy when praised and depressed when criticized, we will surely be miserable.

Once, the Angel of Death went to Earth to tell people when they would die. He met Chen, who was on his way home upon retiring from his job, and said, "You have only three more months to live. I will be at your home in three months and ring my bell. Once you hear the ringing, you will die, as I have directed." The Angel of Death then turned around and spoke to businessman Wang, "You also have only three months to live. I will come to your house in three months to ring my bell, and you will die upon hearing the ringing."

On hearing the news, both of them were petrified. From that day onward, Chen became deeply troubled. Every time he thought of the remaining days in his life, he could not eat or sleep. He sat there and stared at all the money he had made in his lifetime and counted every dollar and cent he had earned with his blood and sweat. He was completely baffled as to what he should do next.

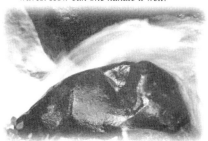

Human life is like the rise and fall of waves. How can one handle it well?

Wang, on the other hand, upon learning that he only had three more months to live, fully understood the brevity of life. He realized that even though he might possess a great fortune, the money was of no use to him at all. He then gave generously to the poor and needy, and began building bridges and repairing roads in the neighborhood to benefit the community. He was so busy with his charity projects that he forgot about his destiny.

When the three months' time was up, the Angel of Death first went to Chen's house. Chen was so depressed and weakened by his worries that upon seeing the Angel of Death, he dropped dead right away without even hearing the bell ring. But Wang had done so much charity work that the whole community decided to award him a huge plaque for his generosity. During the ceremony, drums and gongs were sounded as the crowd cheered. It was so noisy that no matter how loudly the Angel of Death rang his bell, Wang could not hear it and continued to live happily, deeply appreciative of the joy of giving.

Therefore, the future of our lives, including all its gains and losses, pain and joy, are all in our own hands. We should be responsible for our lives!

Learning to Accept

Being born into this world, the most important thing for us to learn is to be polite and well-mannered toward others. As we grow older, we learn different skills and knowledge. In reality, what is even more important is that we learn "to accept," because that is the basis of success in whatever we do.

If we visit a school and observe the students, if they are clipping their nails, sharpening their pencils, flipping through their books, turning about or looking around, and maybe even writing notes to one another during class, then their actions are signs of inattentiveness. They are not paying attention to what the teacher is teaching. Such young learners are not used to accepting and, should they go on to study further or take any kind of formal exams, it would be difficult for them to get any good results.

The same can be said of a vessel for water; if it is leaky, dirty, or overturned, it will be impossible for it to hold any water. Likewise, it is similar to planting seeds. When they are planted on top of the soil, birds come to eat them, and when they are planted among rocks or thorny bushes, they are unable to grow. Therefore, when there is no soil to accept the seeds or no vessel to accept the water, all is wasted. Similarly, if we do not accept the rain from the sky or the warmth of the sunshine, there is nothing anyone can do to help.

A bridge does not prevent someone from crossing it

In the process of learning, whether a student is willing to learn depends on if he/she can accept. When toddlers start to talk, they do so by repeatedly imitating others. So, in learning, accepting is an important step. Not only is it important to learn to accept, but as long as what is learnt is good, we should also accept when conditions are restrictive and unreasonable. If we are able to accept even under adverse circumstances, then we will surely be able to accept when conditions are free and democratic and easy for us to follow the truth.

Regrettably, young people nowadays do not know how to accept. Whether it be the words of their parents or the teachings at school, it seems that nothing can enter their minds because they do not accept. The Buddha's teachings in the *Sutra of Bequeathed Teachings* state, "I am like a doctor prescribing the right medicine for different sicknesses; if you do not take it, then it is not the doctor's fault. I also am like a guide showing you the right path; if you do not follow, then it is not the guide's fault."

The Honorable Ananda was the foremost in listening to the Dharma, and his wisdom came from "the Dharma that is like a flowing ocean, flowing into Ananda's mind." Confucius' disciple Yan Hui was intelligent and learned because he held the belief that "should one learn the truth in the morning, he could die in the evening with no regrets." If someone is able to accept the wise words and teachings of parents, teachers, and the sages, and take them as one's paradigm, then success is ensured, because one will have embraced a myriad of knowledge and wisdom within. Therefore, we should accept all right, pure, benevolent, and truthful knowledge and skills. If you are willing to accept what is good, then you are able to pass down the light to future generations and repay society. Learning to accept is indeed important!

Life is Like a Ball

How can life be symbolized? Some say life is like a dream, others say life is a play, or life is like dew. Then there are those who say that life is suffering, a traveler, or floating clouds! If life can really be symbolized in these ways, this then life is truly sad! Realistically speaking, life is impermanent and has no self, because within the several decades of human life, we are born empty-handed and die in the same manner. If life in this world is spent without cultivating merit, establishing morals, or writing ideas, without leaving any kind of meaning behind, then life is genuinely "coming and going empty-handed!"

So what is life really like? Let us not be too pessimistic about it and instead, follow the middle path; life is like a ball! From the young age of entering school to starting a career, until marriage and raising a family, parents are like a basketball in the eyes of their children. Just like in a basketball game, each player goes after the ball crying, "My ball!" But as parents get old, their children may then start to shun the responsibility of looking after their welfare. The eldest child may start by saying it is not his turn, the second one may then shove it to the third one, and so on. The poor parents may end up moving from household to household, much like a volleyball being bounced around from here to there during a game.

When parents are sick and old, their lot may become like a ball in a soccer game, because their children are so busy with their careers and making money. They may find their parents to be a burden on their sched-ules and want to kick them, as they would the ball, to a distance. In real-ity, parents need not be like the ball in a volleyball or soccer game. As long as they possess morals, knowledge, and savings, they can become the ball in a rugby game. They will find it difficult to move too far, for their children may hold onto them tightly, refusing to let go!

What is life like? If you live your life like the Buddhas and bod-hisattvas, then everyone will respect and admire you. On the other hand, if you transform yourself into the devil, then everyone will surely desert you! Therefore, we can live our lives like "earth," to carry all things; like "heaven," to cover the populace; like "fields of merit" for others to cultivate on; and like a "wisdom bank" for others to draw on endlessly. We therefore need not speak of life as being pitiful. So what is life like? Shouldn't life also be like spring breezes or the winter sun?

If you live your life like the Buddhas and bodhisattvas, then everyone will respect and admire you

Magnanimity

Human beings are by nature all different. We are different in age, gender, ethnicity, religious belief, ideology, occupation, interests, and hobbies. However, despite the uniqueness of each individual person, we cannot overlook the fact that each and every one of us is closely connected in a vast web of interpersonal relationships. A relationship of mutual dependency exists among all the world's people. Therefore, to have magnanimity is to accept the differences as well as the truth that all are essential to our core existence. Without the acknowledgement of the human other, we will live in oblivion. Our lives will be without meaning. For according to the Buddha's teachings, without the proper causes and conditions, nothing will ever come to be.

In order to have greatness, one must be generous and forbearing. An ocean will not be an ocean without the ability to receive all the world's rivers. Emptiness will not be emptiness without the ability to contain all the phenomena of the universe. Nobleness will not be nobleness without the ability to accept and appreciate that which is different. In a world of interpersonal relationships, modesty and magnanimity are the best antidotes to power struggles and obstructions. Hence, to have true respect for one another is to forgive what others have intentionally or unintentionally done wrong.

To have tolerance is the best method to promote world peace; to have magnanimity is the quickest way to broaden one's horizons. Since no one is without fault, we must learn to forbear other's mistakes. We must learn to praise what is good in the character of others and not focus our attention on excessive criticism. Rejection is not a one-way street, for when we reject others for their mistakes, they will do the same for our wrongdoings. Therefore, the only way to a peaceful coexistence is to forgive and forget. We cannot become slaves to our detestation. We will be miserable if all we have is disgust and loathing for our fellow human beings.

Tolerance and forbearance are two of the most important ingredients in our interactions with others because "one must always strive to do the hardest thing and be with the most difficult person." Magnanimity is the highest virtue in interpersonal relationships. We must cultivate our minds to be tolerant of everything and everyone under the sun. We must be like the ocean and the earth in that we reject nothing and accept everything graciously.

As reasonable human beings, we cannot possibly force others to be like us because "there are many doors of expediency for the many temperaments." As noble human beings, we cannot possibly force others to follow our will, for like the five sensory organs, each must function properly to constitute a whole person. The national transportation network will not reach its maximum capacity if trucks, trains, ships, and airplanes do not work together as a team. Therefore, the "division of labor and cooperation" is the key to accomplishing something worthwhile and meaningful.

If the mind is broad without boundaries, it can receive the entire cosmos and beyond. If the mind is narrow and limited, it will not hold a grain of rice. If a person's mind can hold a family, he will become the head of the family. If a person's mind can hold a city, he will become the mayor. If a person's mind can hold a nation, he will become the president. However, if a person can expand his mind to hold the universe and more, he will rediscover his Buddha Nature and be like the Buddha himself.

There is no division between you and me; there is no division between the world and us. The "I" is a part of the human other, who is also a part of the "I." The "I" is a part of the universe, which is also a part of the "I." Since we are all a part of one another, we must treat each other as if we are one and the same; there should be no differentiation. If we want peace in the world and harmony in our relationships, we must learn to identify the "self" with the human other. Only when we can see others as ourselves will we not be tempted to push "ourselves" over the cliff with harmful words and deeds.

The ocean is vast because it welcomes even the smallest stream

Mind Management

"Management" is a very popular subject today. We have business management, financial management, hospital management, and hotel and restaurant management. However, most of us have forgotten the most important subject of "self management," especially "mind management." The "mind" is the root of everything. If we overlook the root and only take care of the branches, how can we expect our lives to be completely fulfilled? Therefore, we must first discipline the mind and steer it in the right direction. Only when the mind is set in the right frame, can everything else fall in the right place. Only when the mind is pure, can everything else be purified. Only when the mind is virtuous and sound, can everything else be likewise

In establishing the teachings, the Buddha advocated mental discipline. "It is for the sake of calming the mind that the Buddha has dispersed the Dharma. If there were no minds, there would be no need for the Dharma." Selfishness is a common human characteristic, but without a way of eradicating it, how can we achieve the ideal of "the world is for all"? Jealousy is a trait shared by all humans, but without a way of controlling it, how can we treat others with sincerity and trust?

The mind is often polluted with prejudice, ignorance, inflexibility, distorted flattery, greed, and unfounded pride, which are the causes of all illness. How could such a mind be of service to the public? How could such a mind shoulder the responsibility of bringing benefits to the world? Therefore, we must discipline the mind and rid it of all defilements.

Throughout his teachings, the Buddha repeatedly describes the mind to be like a monkey, a cow, or a thief. It is restless like a monkey and charges ahead like a mad cow. It steals another's merit like a thief and disregards one's favorable conditions. In order to rid ourselves of our mental flaws, we must learn to bring our minds under control. We must learn to recognize the nature of our minds and be aware of our mental activities, because in a blink of the eye, countless thoughts have come and gone.

As the sayings go, "If the upper beam is not straight, the lower ones will go aslant," and "A fish will begin to stink at its head." If the mind is not properly disciplined, how can it be the leader of the eyes, the ears, the nose, the tongue, and the body? How can we expect the five senses to be good and sound? If we cannot efficiently control our minds and bodies, how in the world can we manage another's affairs?

A mind is like a factory. If it is run well, it will produce good products. If it is badly managed, it will produce pollution. Although managing a factory is difficult, managing the mind is nearly impossible without the Buddha's teachings of precepts, contemplation, and complete wisdom. It is only through the Dharma that we can successfully control the mind.

Our mind is also like a king. If it is benevolent, it will bring benefits to its subjects. If it is tyrannical, it will only bring harm to its people. The mind is also like a skillful artist who can draw anything imaginable. Although it is difficult to discipline the mind, harder than the study of any academic subject, it will become less burdensome with the practice of meditation.

In order to be successful in the subject of mental discipline or "mind management," we must not rely on others, but ourselves. We must elevate our sincerity, our kindness, our compassion, our confidence, our loyalty, and our concentration to a whole new level. We must gather and engage all that goodness in handling our environment, our affairs, and ourselves. We must practice meditation and recite the Buddha's name daily. We must reflect and introspect on a regular basis. In everyday life, we must exercise self-restraint and seek to benefit others. We must constantly remind ourselves to do good and be sympathetic to another's joy. We must remain in a state of equanimity at all times. For these are the only ways to bring calm and tranquility to our minds. For these are the prerequisites to a successful completion to life's course of "mind management."

My Favorites

There is a popular saying, "As long as I like it, nothing is impossible!" This is very wrong indeed, and by upholding its spirit many young people become misguided and are led down the path of no return!

As long as I like it—but what if it is wrong? Then a lot of things are not permissible. If you like to kill, can you simply murder people? If you like to steal and rob, is it all right for you to do so? Or, if you like to loiter in the streets all day, can you just spend all your time doing that? Furthermore, if you choose not to honor your parents and harmonize with your friends, would you be able to do that and live in ease?

If what you like to do is immoral, unkind, illicit, and unreasonable, then it is not permissible. These kinds of things are not allowed, whether you like them or not. So to proclaim, "As long as I like it, nothing is impossible!" is using destructive speech. At times, there are things that we do not like to do, but we still have to comply. For instance, we may not enjoy studying or taking a job; but can we just spend our time doing nothing? We may prefer to slack off at work; but could we get away with that? Some of us may like to be dishonest; but is it possible to go about telling lies all the time?

We need to change the thought that "as long as I like it, nothing is impossible" to "as long as what I like to do helps, benefits, and enables others to succeed, then nothing is impossible"; or even to "as long as what I like to do is not objected to, criticized, or reproached by others, then it is all right for me to do so."

The world does not belong to one person, and the community is not the sole property of anyone in particular. The world is shared by all, and the community is owned by all, so everything does not hinge on the likes or dislikes of individuals. Furthermore, what one person likes or dislikes doing is also dependent on the likes or dislikes of others. What we favor should be in accord with morals, within the law, in tune with others, and not against our own conscience or the law of causality. And what we favor should also be positive, for only that which is positive can be something favorite!

Don't Go for Quick Results

In handling our affairs, the people today share one common ill: a lack of depth and a quick satisfaction with shallowness. They advocate "fast food culture" and go for fast results in everything they do. Their refusal to cultivate broadly and deeply in what they undertake makes it difficult for them to realize any great achievement. As in planting a tree, if it is cut down after a year, the wood is only good for burning. If it is chopped down after three years, the timber may be used for making a stool. But, if it grows for at least ten years before being taken down, it can be used as beams and pillars. Therefore, in not going for quick results, we will be able to withstand the tests of time and the elements. In being able to last, we can reach higher and greater goals!

According to a Buddhist sutra, there once was a deluded king who was quite unhappy upon seeing his queen give birth to a tiny baby princess. He wanted his ministers to find a way for his daughter to grow up instantly. A wise minister offered to take the princess abroad in search of a magical growth potion, on the condition that the king would not be allowed to see the princess in the meantime. The king thought that was an excellent idea and happily agreed to the minister's suggestion. Fifteen years later, the minister brought the princess back to the palace. On seeing his beautiful teenage daughter, the king was so pleased that he awarded his minister a great fortune. The ignorant king of course did not realize that there was no magical potion in the world for babies to grow up instantly.

In the Buddha's time, there was a monk called Dravya, who was responsible for the lodgings of traveling monks. Every night he carried a lantern to show the way to those arriving at the monastery after dark. After serving others for thirty years, when he led the way for the monks coming from afar at night, he no longer needed a lantern because his fingers glowed with light. There was also a novice monk named "Fragrant Mouth," who, from the time he was born, had the excellent practice of not speaking any false speech. After thirty years of speaking the truth, his breath was fragrant with a wondrous scent whenever he spoke.

If Dravya did not carry a lantern and serve others for thirty years, how could he possibly emit light? And if Fragrant Mouth did not speak the truth for thirty years, how could he possibly have such fragrant breath? But young people nowadays all wish to finish work by taking one single step, and they tend to deal with any situation with a quick approach. Without following all the right steps and progressing in stages, even if they are able to get instant results, their achievements will not last for long.

Instant noodles may taste good, but they should not be taken as a staple food. The microwave oven is quick and easy in warming up food, but the heat does not last very long. There is no overnight fame and fortune without years of hard work; there are no tall green pines in the forest without the passage of decades. Life is a marathon, and the ones who can last will win the race. Only those who persevere to the finishing line are the ones to savor the cheers and applause of victory!

On Observing Words and Actions

One day the cicada, sparrow, butterfly, bee, and turtle gathered in the garden and shared their thoughts on life. First the cicada pined, "I notice the changes of the seasons even before the autumn wind blows, quietly witnessing impermanence and death." The sparrow then chirped, "Humans die for money and birds die for feed." The butterfly sighed, "One would die for a flower and be a happy ghost." Next, the bee waxed, "After gathering nectar from a hundred flowers, I can't help but wonder who I am working so hard for all year?"

When everyone was busily airing their observations on life, the catcher nearby heard their chattering noises and cast his net, catching all of them in a single spread. Watching at the side, the turtle stuck out his neck to peek around and gloated, "Ill-fate comes from talking too much!" Even before he finished speaking, a young boy nearby shot over a pebble with his slingshot and hit the turtle right on his head. In pain, the turtle retreated into his shell muttering, "Trouble comes from sticking one's neck out."

From this story we can imagine that those from different walks of life—laborers, merchants, farmers, scholars, soldiers, artists, or civil workers—would also have their own observations on life. They would probably have the following dialogue with the government:

The laborers were the first to report, "We are not working for our own benefit. We labor for the good of the country." The government then ordered, "That is the job of laborers, get on with your work!" The merchants followed, "We offer the best price for our merchandise, one price for all." The government then instructed, "Supply sufficient products to ensure that goods are always available." Next the soldiers exclaimed with much bravado, "We are first on the frontline, ready to die for our country!" The government was delighted and replied, "Quick! Go to the frontline and serve your country." The scholars were stirred and chimed, "We are willing to give our all, even our lives." The government praised, "That's the way it should be!"

Even the artists spoke their minds: "We put the best show for everyone with our beautiful voices and wonderful performances." The government immediately responded, "You should put an act together to perform for the soldiers on the frontline." Not willing to take a back seat to this, the farmers offered, "We plant and toil on the land, saving the nation with our cultivation." The government quickly called out, "Spring and summer are the best times to farm for a good harvest." Last but not least, the civil workers observed, "We strive at public affairs as servants of the country." The government replied, "Working nine to five is the way to do it."

From the above observations, we cannot help but wonder if that is simply catching all with a single cast of the net, or killing with one shot? Or, is it sacrificing willingly upon being praised? Let us hope that the catcher would spare his victims, just as the government should truly work for the welfare of its citizens. If we look back at the road we have been on, we will know how to improve ourselves.

If we look back on the track we have been on, we will know how to improve ourselves

Our Beautiful World

Is the world beautiful? It is indeed beautiful! Look at the rambling mountain ranges, the lush green woods, the chirping birds, and the roaming wild animals; nature embraces all that is full of life and energy! See the azure oceans flowing on and beyond, and the setting sun painting the sky and water with all its glory; the myriad scenes of nature are so breathtaking and magnificent to behold!

It is a pleasure to travel on freeways that are wide and smooth, and just as enjoyable to go down small trails that are narrow and winding. In the countryside, the cottages lazily spew smoke, while sheep and cattle graze in the open fields. What a beautiful portrait of the world! In the city, traffic comes and goes as pedestrians go about their way; the prosperous society is filled with energy. In factories, machines are humming as containers loaded with goods are being transported to port for shipping to other regions, a vista of economic prosperity.

In schools, there are the sounds of students enthusiastically reciting their lessons or vigorously singing songs, a picture of social harmony that is ever so engaging. Members of a family leave early in the morning and return in the evening, like birds back to their nest, when everyone gathers around to exchange the day's happenings, filled with love and respect for one another. It is truly home sweet home!

When we have sumptuous food for our daily meals, we should be mindful of their availability; and when our food is bland and simple, we should practice the Buddhist view of "be it salty or bland, either is as savory." When others show us respect, we remain humble; when met with cold shoulders, we should learn from the Chan masters, "Be it prospering, be it waning, let it be."

When we are traveling and have the chance to stay in large hotels, we consider ourselves in heaven; but when we find ourselves accommodated in a small and dirty cottage, we should be equally as content for having a place to stay. With beneficial friends, we view them as saints and sages deserving of our respect, and with bad ones we take them as mirrors in life to reflect our own behavior.

In life we should have certain hobbies so that sometimes we can paint a picture, or plant a garden; or in our leisure we can take a walk in the park, call up a friend, volunteer to serve others, and be enthusiastic about social service. What harmony and ease that is! When others praise us, we should be appreciative of their kindness and be humble about it as well; and when others criticize us, we should be thankful for their advice and learn from them. If we view everything positively, then the world will be really beautiful!

In reality, we should look beyond the external beauty of the world. We should also build up a wonderful world inside our hearts! When our hearts are beautiful, then the whole world is beautiful: our eyes see beautiful views, our ears hear beautiful words, and our minds think beautiful thoughts. Just as the *Vimalakirti Sutra* says, "A pure mind brings forth a pure land." And the *Avatamsaka Sutra* says, "The heart is a painter that can create all things." All phenomena are created by the mind, so it is imperative that we have a kind, beneficial, and good heart. In this beautiful world and beautiful life, why don't we craft our own beautiful world inside our hearts?

Plywood Philosophy

The most-used construction material today is probably plywood. We can use it as room partitions, doors, ceilings, or even for tabletops and other furniture. Plywood has become an integral part of today's building materials.

A piece of plywood is made up of three layers, with a layer of wood chips pressed together in between two pieces of strong thin boards. It contains recycled and leftover wood. In this world, the capable can create miracles out of garbage and are able to reuse waste material. For instance, a capable officer can turn defeated soldiers into brave warriors; a good doctor can create a remedy out of dry wood and stones; an able blacksmith can forge steel out of rusted iron; and a skillful homemaker can cook a gourmet dish from leftovers.

Plywood is a very useful material, and it can even be painted different colors so that it can be both sturdy and good-looking. In this world, relying on one factor alone in order to achieve success in anything we set out to do is often not good enough. We need two, three, four, or even multiple causes and conditions before we can accomplish a task.

Even though many advocate single living for both men and women, it seems that there are few who are truly happy with their lifestyles. In finding the other half, women usually look for men with a sense of heroism, good looks, philosophical thinking, and a saintly personality. Their financial condition, academic achievement, and family background should also be outstanding. Such is the combination of multiple causes and conditions, just like the multiple functions of plywood.

As for men, living without the other half is not easy either. A house without a mistress is not quite a home; a man needs a woman to look after his daily needs. He also looks for a woman with multiple qualities like "plywood," someone who is good-looking, gentle, elegant, and personable. In addition, she should be knowledgeable and a capable housekeeper. It takes the combination of many causes and conditions in order to become a piece of plywood.

As humans, we all have needs, but there should not be too many either. To have just one is too little, and asking for too much becomes a burden to others. Therefore, men and women should not demand too much from one another. The philosophy of plywood could also be applied to life and society. In relating to our country, the community, and even our family and friends, we naturally have demands of them, but there should not be too many. Plywood is good because it is just right, but if you require more than that, then you should only demand more of yourself. The world is filled with a myriad of phenomena, so as we interact with them, let us just be a piece of plywood!

The capable can create miracles out of garbage and are able to reuse waste material

Practice Filial Piety Here and Now

There was once a little frog that had always contradicted his mother's orders. When she asked him to go east, he would go west, and vice versa. One day, the mother frog realized that she was going to die soon. She wanted to be buried in the mountains and not near the water. But since the little frog always contradicted her wishes, she thought she would tell him to bury her near the water. However, the little frog had awakened from his mistakes and decided to oblige his mother's last wishes. So he buried her near the water. In the evenings, he worried about his mother being too lonely by the water, so he croaked loudly there. When it rained, he worried that the rising water would wash her away. Again, he croaked loudly by the water. However, when his mother was alive he would not listen to her, so what purpose does all the sadness and croaking serve upon her death?

In today's society, fewer and fewer people practice filial piety, creating problems associated with the "generation gap." Nowadays, the different generations have become more and more indifferent toward one another. In hospitals, one can easily observe that there are many filial, pious parents in the children's ward, while there are few filial, pious children in the geriatric ward. Many children do not care enough to visit their parents in the hospital, much less attend to every need of their bedridden seniors. In our daily lives, we observe parents who unconditionally take their children to and from school day in and day out without a second thought. But when children are occasionally required to accompany their parents to medical appointments, they get impatient and behave as if they are doing their parents a huge favor.

The love of parents for their children is illustrated by the following verse, "I can still remember how I brought up my child, and now my child is bringing up my grandchild. It is alright if my child lets me go hungry, but hopefully my grandchild will never let my child go hungry." There was once a butcher in Mount Putuo who treated his mother very poorly. One day, he went with others for a pilgrimage up the mountain. On learning about the existence of a living "Avalokitesvara" Bodhisattva, he started to ask around for her whereabouts. An old monk then told him, "The living 'Avalokitesvara' is already living in your home." On rushing home, he discovered that the monk was referring to his mother, who explained, "When you do not even honor your parents at home, what is the use of making a pilgrimage up the mountain?"

In honoring our parents, we should not wait until they are gone. We should do it here and now! Otherwise, we will be like the little frog croaking loudly by the water.

To use all our heart to return even a small favor

Practice What We Preach

"To speak of the Way for a mile is not as effective as practicing it for a foot." Some of us can speak eloquently and are even quite learned. However, simply being articulate in what we know without practicing it renders all the words empty and useless.

Once, there were two devotees who wanted to pay a pilgrimage to Mount Putuo. Chen was a poor man, so he walked all the way there after he made the decision. Wang, on the other hand, was wealthy. He thought he had all the time and money he needed, so he could fly there when he had the time to do so. Half a year later, though he walked all the way, Chen had returned from his pilgrimage, but Wang had not even started on his trip. If we want to reach a goal, just talking about it without any action never accomplishes anything. We must act appropriately in order to realize our purpose. So instead of sitting there talking, we should get up and do it.

There were a few popular slogans in China at one time. "Chinese only talk and do not do," "Germans do as they talk," "Americans do and do not talk," while "Developing countries do not talk nor do." It's a small wonder that there are both strong and weak countries in the world. The reason for that can be accounted for by the characteristics of their citizens, as well as their attitudes toward speech and action. For those who practice what they say, anything can be accomplished.

The ancients were quick in observing the strengths and weaknesses of the human world. Be it progress or digress, they provided us with guidelines all along. The Buddha told us to "understand as well as practice." Chinese scholar Wang Yangming encouraged us to "combine knowledge and practice." Dr. Sun Yat-sen observed that "It is easier to practice than to be knowledgeable." However, we do not appreciate the subtleties therein. We all learn to "talk but not do." So, we are all responsible for the state of our nation.

Once there was a young man who wanted to become world-famous overnight, but never really worked toward his goal. One day, he met the great inventor Thomas Edison. He hastily went up to ask Edison how to become famous. Perfectly aware of the young man's problem, Edison replied, "Wait till you are dead, then you will be famous." Puzzled, the young man asked, "Why wait till after death to be famous?" Edison explained, "Because you want to own a mansion now but you never take any action to build it. The mansion will not appear out of thin air. So if you live your entire life dreaming, after your death, people will mention your name as a lesson to those who dream all the time and do not do any work. You will therefore fulfill your wish to become world-famous."

Just talking about food brings no satisfaction, just as a picture of a cake eases no hunger. If we want to get rich or be strong, then we should practice what we say because practicing is superior to just talking.

Prescription for the Heart

On the back cover of the Chinese version of *Humble Table, Wise Fare* is a "prescription for life," emulating Chan Master Shitou's "prescription for the heart." It is as follows:

A piece of good heart, a section of compassion, several ounces of good reasoning, ten grains of respect, a chunk of morality, one honest fruit, and ten folds of integrity; in addition, other important ingredients are faith and practice, complete openness, and lots of convenience. All these ingredients should be first mixed together in the pot of magnanimity, then stewed in the oven of big heartedness. Do not sear, do not char, reduce to low heat to control the temper, then grind it up in the bowl of teamwork. Using careful thinking as a base, encouragement as pills, we should take it three times daily, at anytime of the day, together with the soup of caring. If we can do this, then we can rid ourselves of all ailments.

When our heart is ill, sometimes it gets frustrated; at other times it becomes delusional. It then may become filled with greed or full of unceasing anger. When our body is sick, we can use physiotherapy, medication, special diets, or even exercise. However, if the heart is ill, then how should we treat it? Buddhism refers to the Buddha as the "Master Doctor," the Dharma as medicine for the heart, and monastics as nurses.

For most, it is not difficult to detect a sickness of the body, for there are always instruments for diagnosis. But when the heart is sick, it will not be easy to discover; or even when the problem is found, it is not easy to cure completely. For instance, consider the illnesses of suspicion, arrogance, hatred, deviance, hypocrisy, worries, or even shamelessness, slothfulness, and indolence; without the Buddha's prescription for the heart, how can our sickness possibly be cured? The dust and sickness in our hearts are varied, and Buddhism offers many different prescriptions for them. For instance, the sickness of greed is to be treated with generosity, anger with compassion, ignorance with wisdom, arrogance with humility, suspicion with right faith, and deviance with right path.

A Buddhist sutra says, "The heart takes on the hell realm, takes on the animal realm, and takes on the heaven and human realms." The three suffering realms as well as other realms are realized upon one single thought of our heart. Since all ailments derive from the existence of the heart, the prescription for the heart is even more important for us commoners who crave the pleasures of the five senses and the six dusts of the human world.

Do you take the Buddha's prescription for the heart daily?

Pride and Arrogance

Pride and arrogance seem to be similar in what they connote. But when we explore further, the difference is obvious. Arrogance is the enemy of success, but pride is its friend. To be arrogant brings about others' contempt, but to have pride earns us their respect.

Some people think they know it all and behave arrogantly. Or, they may have earned themselves some fame and fortune and think they own the world. Due to their arrogance, others view them with disdain. On the other hand, some people may be down to their last penny but they never beg for mercy. Though they do not have any worldly possessions, their pride earns them the respect of others. So, if the rich and famous are not arrogant, and the poor can hold their heads high and proud, then everyone can be happy with their lives.

Nobody likes an arrogant person. However, there are some who enjoy being servile to the rich and are obsequious to them, regardless of how obnoxious the latter is in their arrogance. Those who have pride would rather be in the company of the same. They find joy in sharing their ideals and outlooks about life.

There are so many who fail because of their arrogance. An arrogant general will surely lose the battle if that is his attitude in leading his troops. Similarly, an arrogant teacher will lose good connections with his or her students. By the same token, an arrogant supervisor will lose the trust of subordinates. Arrogance will also break up any beautiful friendship. But if arrogance is replaced by pride, then a person will earn the respect of everyone.

In history, there are many examples where arrogance brought down kings and emperors. Their hard-earned kingdoms toppled with them and they left behind only notoriety in the history books. But those who lived with pride and stood up to the tests of their times set examples for generations to come. Arrogance and pride; they lead us down very different paths in life.

People become arrogant when things go well and depressed when they are down in life. However, we should rid ourselves of any arrogance, and maintain our pride even when we are not doing as well. As the saying goes, "One's integrity should never be compromised by wealth, poverty, or force."

Arrogance and pride are the result of comparisons. We compare our strengths and weaknesses with the abilities and shortcomings of others. Some compare their strengths with the shortcomings of others and feed their arrogance on that. But others compare their weaknesses with the abilities of others, igniting their will to strive on.

While we should not be arrogant because arrogance only brings us failure, we should also be aware that excessive pride will not help us progress in life either. So, in hard times, we should maintain our pride by not coveting fame and fortune. In good times, we will not breed arrogance by bearing in mind the times of hardship. If we can balance life in this way, then we can live in harmony and self-respect.

Arrogance and pride are the result of comparisons.

Arrogance and pride are the result of comparison

Glossary

Amitabha Buddha: The Buddha of Infinite Light or Infinite Life. Amitabha is one of the most popular Buddhas in Mahayana Buddhism. He presides over the Western Pure Land.

Aniruddha: One of the ten great disciples of the Buddha. He is known as the foremost in divine-eye.

Arhat: In Pali, "arahat." Literally, "being worthy of." One who has eliminated all afflictions and passions, which will never arise again.

Avalokitesvara Bodhisattva: Literally, "He who hears the sounds of the world." In Mahayana Buddhism, Avalokitesvara is known as the Bodhisattva of Compassion. He can manifest himself in any form necessary in order to help any being. He is considered one of the great bodhisattvas in Mahayana Buddhism.

Avatamsaka Sutra: Translated in English as The *Flower Ornament Scriptures*; in Chinese, *Huayan Jing*. It is one of the major texts in Mahayana Buddhism. This sutra is the first teaching expounded by the Buddha after his enlightenment.

Bodhgaya: A city in Bihar, India, near the Nairanjana River. It is the place where Sakyamuni Buddha achieved enlightenment.

Bodhicitta: The mind seeking to achieve enlightenment.

Bodhisattva: Literally, "enlightening being." Anyone who seeks Buddhahood and vows to liberate all sentient beings. Buddha: Literally, "awakened one." When "the Buddha" is used, it usually refers to the historical Buddha, Sakyamuni Buddha.

Buddha Nature: The inherent nature that exists in all beings. It is the capability to achieve Buddhahood.

Buddhahood: The attainment and expression that characterizes a Buddha. Buddhahood is the highest goal of all beings.

Cause and Condition: Referring to the primary cause (cause) and the secondary causes (conditions). The seed out of which a plant or a flower grows is a good illustration of a primary cause; the elements of soil, humidity, sunlight, and so forth, could be considered secondary causes.

Cause and Effect: The most basic doctrine in Buddhism, which explains the formation of all relations and connections in this world.

Chan: The Chinese translation of the Sanskrit (Skt.) term, dhyana; it refers to meditative concentration.

Confucianism: The philosophy named after Confucius. It was the official philosophy of China, established in the third century B.C.E.

Confucius: (551-479 B.C.E) In Chinese, "Kung Tzu." He was an early Chinese moral philosopher.

Cultivation: Synonymous with "practice." Cultivation is the training of heart and mind in generosity, virtue, calmness, wisdom, etc.

Daoan: (312-385 C.E.) One of China's greatest Buddhist preachers, famous for his ability to speak about the Dharma.

Daoxin: The Fourth Patriarch of Chan in China.

Dharani: Also known as "mantra" or "spell." Literally, it means "uniting and holding," which further extends to "uniting all dharmas and holding all meanings."

Dharma: With a capital "D": 1) the ultimate truth and 2) the teachings of the Buddha. When the Dharma is applied or practiced in life, it is 3) righteousness or virtues. With a lowercase "d": 4) anything that can be thought of, experienced, or named; close to "phenomena."

Dharma joy: The joy that arises in the mind after listening to or learning the Buddha's teachings.

Diamond Sutra: The *Vajracchedika Prajna Paramita Sutra*. The *Diamond Sutra* sets forth the doctrine of emptiness and the perfection of wisdom. It is named such because the perfection of wisdom cuts delusion like a diamond.

Dravya: Full name: "Dravya-malla-putra." One of the Buddha's disciples who became a novice monk at fourteen years of age and attained arhatship at sixteen. He was good at making tools, building houses, and general construction.

Eighty-four thousand troubles: In Buddhism, "eighty-four thousand" is a way to describe "many"; "troubles" is synonymous with "afflictions." Therefore, "eighty-four thousand troubles" indicates that sentient beings have many afflictions, which are due to greed, hatred, and ignorance.

Emptiness: Skt. "sunyata." A fundamental Buddhist concept, also known as non-substantiality or relativity, meaning all phenomena have no fixed or independent nature. In Buddhism, it can be divided into two categories: 1) associated with individuals and called "non-substantiality of persons" and 2) associated with phenomena and called "non-substantiality of dharmas." Therefore, the concept of emptiness is related to dependent origination and impermanence.

Five Aggregates: "Five Skandhas." They represent the composition of body and mind. The five skandhas are form, feeling, perception, mental formations, and consciousness.

Fo Guang Shan: The monastic order in Kaoshiung, Taiwan, established by Venerable Master Hsing Yun in 1964.

Four Great Elements: The four basic constituents of matter: 1) Earth (solid matter), 2) water (liquid), 3) fire (heat), and 4) wind (energy).

Four meditation stages: In the first stage, one is beyond the realm of desire. In this meditative state, the mind is joyful and tranquil. In the second stage, the mind is even and calm. Bliss is born in this state of concentration. In the third stage, there is no clinging. The mind is filled with joy, but there is no attachment. In the fourth stage, there is complete freedom of all thought-consciousness. This stage is beyond joy, and it is the purest of all four dhyanas (states of meditative concentration).

Guan Yin: Also known as "Kuan Yin." The Chinese name for Avalokitesvara Bodhisattva.

Guishan: (771-853 C.E.) Also known as Guishan Lingyou, he was the founder of the Guiyang sect. He encountered and learned much from Hanshan and Shide (see endnotes) and later studied with Master Baizhang, becoming his chief disciple. His work is entitled *Sayings of Chan Master Guishan Lingyou*.

Hanshan: A hermit in the Chinese Tang Dynasty. The Chinese term "hanshan" means "Cold Mountain." He is named such because he lived in a cold cave close to Mount Tiantai. According to legend, he was the manifestation of Manjusri Bodhisattva. He completed the literary work The *Poems of Hanshan*, which includes over three hundred poems.

Heart Sutra: One of the most important sutras in Mahayana Buddhism. It is regarded as the essence of Buddhist teachings and is chanted daily in communities all over the world.

Huiyuan: (334-416 C.E.). Also known as Lushan Huiyuan, he was the First Patriarch of the Chinese Pure Land School. He and his younger brother, Huichi, became Master Daoan's disciples after listening to him discourse on the wisdom sutras.

Impermanence: One of the most basic truths taught by the Buddha. It is the concept that all conditioned dharmas, or phenomena, will arise, abide, change, and disappear due to causes and conditions.

Karma: This means, "work, action, or deeds" and is related to the law of cause and effect. All deeds, whether good or bad, produce effects. The effects may be experienced instantly or they may not come into fruition for many years or even many lifetimes.

Ksana: In Buddhism, a ksana is the shortest measure of time. Sixty ksana are equal to approximately one finger-snap.

Mahabodhi Temple: Skt. "Mahabodhi-samgharama." It is located north of the bodhi tree in Bodhgaya, India, where Sakyamuni Buddha attained enlightenment. The temple, which still stands, was built by a Burmese king during the twelfth or thirteenth century.

Mahakasyapa: One of the ten great disciples of the Buddha. He is known as the foremost in the practice of asceticism and was regarded as the chief of the order. In Chan, he is considered the First Patriarch of Dharma Transmission, due to the experience of smiling and becoming enlightened when Sakyamuni Buddha held up a flower.

Maitreya: The Future Buddha. It is said that he currently presides over Tusita Heaven, where he is expounding the Dharma to heavenly beings in the inner palace.

Mount Putuo: One of the four most famous mountains in China, located in Zhejiang Province. It is considered the sacred mountain of Avalokitesvara Bodhisattva.

Mount Tai: A famous mountain located in Shandong Province, China.

Novice: Monks and nuns who have not yet received full ordination. In Sanskrit, "sramaneraka" is a male novice; "sramanerika" is a female novice. In Pali, they are "sramanera" and "sramaneri."

Prajna: Literally, "wisdom." Prajna is the highest form of wisdom. In Buddhism, it is the third of Three Studies, which include precepts, concentration, and wisdom. It is also the last of the six perfections, called prajnaparamita. Prajna is the wisdom of insight into the true nature of all phenomena, arising from the practice of the Eightfold Noble Path and the six perfections.

Prasenajit: The King of the Kausala and Kasi Kingdoms. He was the Buddha's contemporary and a faithful follower of the Buddha as well as a supporter of the Sangha.

Precepts: Skt. "Sila." The rules of conduct and discipline established by the Buddha.

Sage: Sage usually refers to arhats, bodhisattvas, or Buddhas. The difference between ordinary people and sages is that sages are able to always keep their minds pure, unmoved, empty, and still.

Sakyamuni Buddha: (581-501 B.C.E.) The historical founder of Buddhism He was born the Prince of Kapilavastu, son of King Suddhodana. At the age of twenty-nine, he left the royal palace and his family to search for the meaning of existence. At the age of thirty-five, he attained enlightenment under the bodhi tree. He then spent the next forty-five years expounding his teachings, which include the Four Noble Truths, the Eightfold Path, the Law of Cause and Effect, and Dependent Origination. At age eighty, he entered the state of parinirvana.

Sengcan: (?-606 C.E.) He was the Third Patriarch of Chinese Chan School and received the transmission of the Dharma from the Second Patriarch, Huike. He was also the teacher of Chan Master Daoxin. He wrote a work entitled *Xin Xin Ming*.

Shide: A hermetic monk who lived in the Guoqing Temple at Mount Tiantai during the Chinese Tang Dynasty. He was reared by Chan Master Fenggan, who also served as his teacher and master. He was also closely connected to Hanshan. Shide, Hanshan, and Chan Master Fenggan were given the title "Three Sages" or "Three Hermits at Guoqing." According to legend, Fenggan was the manifestation of Amitabha Buddha, Hanshan was the manifestation of Samantabhadra Bodhisattva.

Shitou: (700-790 C.E.). Also known as Shitou Xiqian, he was one of the great Chan Masters in the Chinese Tang Dynasty. He was a student of Master Huineng and Master Qingyuan Xingsi.

Six Realms: The various modes of existence in which rebirth occurs, ranging from the lower realms of hell, hungry ghosts, and animals to the higher realms of humans, asura, and heaven.

Six-syllable Dharani: "Om Mani Padme Hum," also known as the dharani of Avalokitesvara Bodhisattva. Originally, it was widely recited by Tantric Buddhists, but it gradually became a popular dharani to recite among Buddhists from many different schools.

Su Dongpo: (1038-1101 C.E.) Also called Su Shi, he was a famous scholar and poet during the Chinese Song Dynasty.

Sun Yat-sen: (1866-1925 C.E.) The father of the Republic of China.

Sutra: Literally, "threaded together." The scriptures directly taught by the Buddha.

Sutra of Bequeathed Teachings: This sutra describes the Buddha's last teachings before he entered parinirvana. The teachings instruct the disciples to follow the pratimoksa (precepts), see it as the teacher, and rely on it for controlling the five sense organs, attaining freedom from hatred and arrogance, and maintaining a diligent practice.

Sutra of Contemplation of Amatiyus: Also known as *Sutra of Contemplation of Amatiyus*. Skt. *Amitayurdhyana Sutra*. It is one of three Pure Land sutras. Its content describes the Western Pure Land and teaches how to be reborn there, including cultivating the three merits and the ten wholesome conducts, upholding the precepts, and contemplating the Western Pure Land and Amitabha Buddha.

Sutra of Sixteen Contemplations: Also known as *Sutra of Contemplation of Amatiyus*. It is named such because in this sutra, sixteen methods of contemplating the Western Pure Land and Amitabha Buddha are provided.

Ten Directions: In Buddhism, this term is used to refer to everywhere, indicating the eight points of the compass (north, west, east, south, southeast, southwest, northeast and northwest) plus the zenith and nadir.

The Book of Odes: The oldest collection of poetry and songs in Chinese history, completely edited during the time period known as the Epoch of Spring and Autumn (770-403 B.C.). It contains 305 poems and songs, which are classified into three categories.

The Way to the Buddhahood: In Chinese, *Cheng Fo Zhi Dao*. It was written by Venerable Yin-shun, translated by Dr. Wing H. Yeung, and published by Wisdom Publications in 1998.

Three Realms: The realms where sentient beings reside and transmigrate, including the sense-desire realm, the realm of form, and the realm of formlessness.

Triple Gem: Also known as "Triple Jewels" or "Three Jewels." The Triple Gem is the Buddha, the Dharma, and the Sangha.

Vimalakirti Sutra: Also known as *Vimalakirtinirdesa Sutra*. The main purposes of this sutra are to clarify the methods of practice for liberation that Vimalakirti has achieved and to explain the practices of Mahayana bodhisattvas and the virtues that the layperson should fulfill.

Wang Yangming: (1473-1529 C.E.) One of the Neo-Confucian scholars in China.

Wumen: (1183-1260 C.E.) Also known as Wumen Huikai, he was a Chan Master in the Chinese Song Dynasty. His works include *Sayings of Chan Master Wumen* and *Wumen Guan*.

Xuanzang: (602 -664 C.E.) A great master in the Chinese Tang Dynasty. He is one of four great translators in Buddhist history. He studied in India for seventeen years and was responsible for bringing many collections of works, images, pictures, as well as one hundred and fifty relics to China from India. His famous work is entitled *Buddhist Records of the Western Regions*.

Yan Hui: (521-490 B.C.) Also known as Yen Hui, he was one of Confucius' chief disciples and was praised and respected by Confucius and his other students.

Yellow River Gorge: The second longest river in China. It can be traced to a source high in the majestic Yagradagze Mountains in the nation's far west. It loops north, bends south, and flows east for 5,464 km until it empties into the sea, draining a basin of 745,000 sq km, which nourishes 120 million people. Millennia ago, the Chinese civilization emerged from the central region of this basin.

About

Venerable Master Hsing Yun

Venerable Master Hsing Yun was born in Jiangdu, Jiangsu Province, China, in 1927. Tonsured under Venerable Master Zhikai at age twelve, he became a novice monk at Qixia Vinaya School and Jiaoshan Buddhist College. He was fully ordained in 1941, and is the 48th Patriarch of the Linji (Rinzai) Chan School.

He went to Taiwan in 1949 where he undertook the revitalization of Chinese Mahayana Buddhism on the island with a range of activities novel for its time. In 1967, he founded the Fo Guang Shan (Buddha's Light Mountain) Buddhist Order, and has since established more than a hundred temples in Taiwan and on every continent worldwide. Hsi Lai Temple, the United States Headquarters of Fo Guang Shan, was built outside Los Angeles in 1988.

At present, there are nearly two thousand monks and nuns in the Fo Guang Shan Buddhist Order. The organization also oversees sixteen Buddhist colleges; five publishing houses, including Buddha's Light Publishing and Hsi Lai University Press; four universities, one of which is Hsi Lai University in Los Angeles; two nursing homes for the elderly; a secondary school; a satellite television station; and an orphanage.

A prolific writer and an inspiring speaker, Master Hsing Yun has written many books on Buddhist sutras and a wide spectrum of topics over the past five decades. Most of his speeches and lectures have been compiled into essays defining Humanistic Buddhism and outlining its practice. Some of his writings and lectures have been translated into various languages, such as English, Spanish, German, Russian, Japanese, Korean, etc.

The Venerable Master is also the founder of the Buddha's Light International Association, a worldwide organization of lay Buddhists dedicated to the propagation of Buddhism, with over 130 chapters and a membership of more than a million.

About

Buddha's Light Publishing and
Fo Guang Shan International Translation Center

As long as Venerable Master Hsing Yun has been a Buddhist monk, he has had a strong belief that books and other documentation of the Buddha's teachings unite us emotionally, help us practice Buddhism at a higher altitude, and continuously challenge our views on how we define and live our lives.

In 1996, the Fo Guang Shan International Translation Center was established with this goal in mind. This marked the beginning of a string of publications translated into various languages from the Master's original writings in Chinese. Presently, several translation centers have been set up worldwide. Centers that coordinate translation or publication projects are located in Los Angeles and San Diego, USA; Sydney, Australia; Berlin, Germany; Argentina; South Africa; and Japan.

In 2001, Buddha's Light Publishing was established to publish Buddhist books translated by Fo Guang Shan International Translation Center as well as other valuable Buddhist works. Buddha's Light Publishing is committed to building bridges between East and West, Buddhist communities, and cultures. All proceeds from our book sales support Buddhist propagation efforts.